IN COLD SWEAT

IN COLD SWEAT

Interviews with
Really Scary Musicians

Thomas Wictor

Limelight Editions
New York

First Limelight Edition   July 2001

Manufactured in the United States of America

Library of Congress Cataloging-in-Publication Data

Wictor, Thomas.
   In cold sweat : interviews with really scary musicians / Thomas
   Wictor.-- 1st Limelight ed.
     p. cm.
   Discography: p.
   ISBN 0-87910-956-4
    1. Rock musicians--United States--Interviews. I. Title.

ML394.W53 2001
781.66'092'273--dc21
[B]

                          2001029344

Designed by Mulberry Tree Press, Inc. (www.mulberrytreepress.com)

For Helena

dude, you rock

Contents

Acknowledgments

Thanks to Jim Roberts for making this possible. Thanks to Karl Coryat for his patience, kindness, advice, wisdom, support, and incomparable hands-on approach. Thanks to Greg Olwell for his humor and helpfulness over the years. Thanks to Richard Johnston for pitching in at the last minute. Thanks to the mysterious Martha Lawrence for all that publishing jazz. Thanks to Joe Travers for his assistance. Thanks to Mike Keneally for acting as matchmaker and encyclopedia. Thanks to Arthur Barrow for clearing up that one little thing. Thanks to Neil Zlozower and Jill Furmanovsky for their artistry, generosity, and twice-in-my-lifetime professionalism. Thanks to Louise Nemschoff for the reality checks.

Thanks to Mel Zerman for his suggestions and confidence. Thanks to Kathryn Koldehoff for making me a better writer.

Thanks to John Taylor, catalyst and everlasting bass hero.

Thanks to Theo and Juliet for their friendship, photos, input, entertainment value, and the many, many, many opportunities to burn calories.

Thanks most of all to Gene, Peter, Jerry, and Scott.

*God! Is there anything
uglier than a frightened man?*
—Jean Anouilh

Preface

All my life, I've had one overriding fear. Ever since I can remember, I've been terrified of making a fool out of myself.

I was raised a Catholic, and in our services there's a ritual called "exchanging a sign of peace." Following the lead of the priest, you shake hands with everyone around you and chant, "Peace be with you!" As a seven-year-old upset by the Vietnam War, I was deeply committed to peace, so when the handshaking time came during one mass, I reached out of my pew and patted the back of the man in front of me. He was gigantic and a complete stranger, but since he was there with our neighbors, I knew it was the Christian thing to do. At my touch, he jerked as if I'd goosed his enormous rump. He whirled and gaped down at me, violated to his core. Luckily, no one in my family seemed to have noticed. I was sure that I'd gotten away with it until, in the car on the way home, my father suddenly spluttered, "Did you see that guy's face when Tommy patted his back? Boy, was *he* surprised!"

Another incident, which twenty years later still makes my face burn, occurred the afternoon I was chosen to umpire a Little League game, even though I knew nothing at all about sports. My brother Pat was on a baseball squad, and we'd watch him play on the weekends. This day, the usual second-base umpire was absent, so I was asked to sub. I was in eleventh grade and hadn't even known that there *was* a second-base umpire. My impression was that the guy out on the field was a coach or a chaplain, maybe.

They played for keeps, these Little Leaguers, and their parents backed them with savage gusto. The yelling was constant, most of it supplied by paunchy, apoplectic dads. After about an hour, someone hit a touchdown or whatever, and a kid in the outfield scooped it up and threw it to the first baseman, who stomped on that square bag-thing. I understood that the batter was thus "out." He'd had a teammate on first base, and this boy was now sprinting for second base, behind which I stood. The first baseman lobbed the ball to the second baseman, who caught it and firmly touched the runner on the shoulder with his glove.

Now, I knew that the kid was out, but my aphasic brain apparently didn't because I opened my mouth and called out, "Safe!"

Pandemonium.

The field exploded in piping screams, while behind home plate frenzied parents began tearing at the diamond-link fence. The chief umpire, who was also the principal of my high school, galloped up and cried, "What happened? He didn't make the tag?"

With no idea what that meant, I nodded, thinking of morgue toe tags and how much better I'd feel wearing one. The boss umpire announced that the runner was safe, and the game must resume. All around me, children threw down their gloves and sobbed; men howled profane phrases at the sky; and in the stands, my mother and siblings tried to look as inconspicuous as possible.

Oh, I could go on and on. But I won't. I'll just add one more of my formative experiences.

After I graduated from college, I went to Japan. I'd planned to study finance but never actually got around to it because it was much easier to teach English, drink, and play in a bar band instead. I'd owned an electric bass since I was eighteen, so a model-handsome Canadian guitarist-teacher named Steiv recruited me and a drummer. We christened ourselves A Window and after months of practice began booking dates. On our opening night, the club was packed with three hundred paying customers, most of them our friends and students. When we were announced, I bounded out on stage with my left-handed

Fender Jazz Bass, ready to *rock*. I was all dolled up in basic black, my hair slick with gel, and my glasses hidden in my front pocket. The script called for me to plug in and run the strings of my bass across a microphone stand, duplicating the Hawaiian guitar used in the opening of the *Merrie Melodies* theme song: *Bwuhhhhhhhhhmmm?*

Everything was peachy until I saw the crowd. One look at all those hungry smiles, and I froze. Instantly. I was petrified with stage fright. I managed to perform that night, but I have no memory of it. The only parts of my body I was able to move were my hands, a phenomenon well documented in that every photo taken during the event showed me in exactly the same position. In the weeks following our debut, I was given dozens of identical shots of me gazing at the lead singer, my face wizened and drained of color. Our band played the Tokyo club circuit for three years, and I never overcame my paralysis. Even after three years, I still had the stage presence of a filing cabinet.

That's why I became interested in music journalism. Once I realized that I couldn't be a musician myself, writing about them seemed like the next best thing; so even though I'd never published a word, I submitted an idea to *Bass Player*. A visionary named Jim Roberts approved it without asking a single question about my credits, and I was on my way, I thought.

Well, all these years later, I'm more realistic. It's a tough old world for freelance writers, but since I chose this particular road, I try not to complain publicly. Anyway, it's not important or even interesting how tough it is. What's important to me is that I went ahead despite my stutter, my complete lack of experience and connections, my sense of total fraudulence, and my ever-present fear of screwing up. So, like, it's bitchin' to follow your dreams and stuff.

This book is oral history with a dash of memoir, I suppose. It contains complete documentations of one interviewer's personal experiences with Gene Simmons, Peter Hook, Jerry Casale, and Scott Thunes on particular days. It's not a collection of biographies; nor is it "the definitive" anything. I don't want to tell readers how to interpret the contents, so the only other thing I'll say is this: Almost immediately, I realized that I could ask these guys whatever I wanted. I didn't expect them necessarily to answer, but they made it clear that they wouldn't take offense at my questions. For an entertainment journalist, that's *extremely* liberating because it rarely happens. Artists can take offense at quite a lot, including gender. I was once turned down by a very A-list musician whose people said that she never spoke to male interviewers. Sadly, like a magnesium flare, she burned brightly but oh-so-briefly and no longer attracts attention from any interviewers, male or female. Another time, I was forbidden to ask about *X;* if I did, the session would be terminated and my name added to a blacklist of untrustworthy writers. Most recently, I found out ten minutes into an interview that the musician in question had played on just one of the CD's twelve tracks. When I informed my editor, the band's publicist called and told me that my behavior had been outrageous and disrespectful. There would be repercussions—*major* repercussions.

So being given free rein is very nice, a great compliment or a sign of the artist's utter indifference. It doesn't matter to me which it is, as long as I'm not tossed out of the room.

Finally, if you're wondering why I've included only bassists here, it's because I've pretty much interviewed only bassists. I love the bass, and these are four of my favorite players. They're also the four most complex and intimidating people I've ever met.

It's true that freelance music journalism has brought me no fame and no fortune, but that's okay because I couldn't have handled them anyway. What I *have* gotten is the chance to exorcise a few personal demons, and for that I'm grateful. I can honestly say that these days, I fear (almost) nothing. I could talk to (virtually) anyone now and not worry (that much) about what I did, what I said, or how I came across.

I still don't pat strangers on the back, though, and I stay well away from all baseball games.

IN COLD SWEAT

Part One
Gene Simmons

January 28, 1996

Chapter One

The Doctor Will See You Now

There has never been a more enduring rock band than Kiss. From their first record in 1974, they've defied all predictions about what they'd do next or what was going to happen to them. They've survived the almost universal loathing of music critics, the departure or death of band members, sporadic financial catastrophe, epic personal excesses, and the public's inevitably changing tastes. They even pulled off what may be a first for a rock group: dramatic artistic growth after almost a quarter century of existence. When Gene Simmons gave this interview in 1996, Kiss was finishing a new studio album, *Carnival of Souls.* They seemed ready to reinvent themselves one more time, preparing another of their bold, market-savvy leaps forward. Then they yanked the rug out from under everyone, especially me.

One of the biggest problems Kiss has faced is the distracting bombast of their own makeup, costumes, platform boots, dry ice, fire breathing, blood spitting, explosions, and light shows. The comic-book theatricality makes it easy to forget that the band plays *music* too, music that set the tone for fifteen years. Kiss is *the* premier metal act. It's inarguable. Seventeen of their thirty-one records have gone platinum, double platinum, triple platinum, or quadruple platinum. Most of the rest have gone gold. Musicians ranging from the late godfather of grunge Kurt

Cobain to country megastar Garth Brooks have proclaimed themselves fans. And if that weren't enough, a lot of the songs are just plain good. I defy anyone to listen to "God of Thunder" *(Destroyer)* or "Calling Dr. Love" *(Rock and Roll Over)* without first tapping his or her toes and then humming the melodies. For the next three days.

Gene Simmons is as improbable a metal icon as you could imagine. Born Chaim Witz in Haifa, Israel, the son of a Holocaust survivor, he went to New York in 1958 as a nine-year-old who spoke no English and had never seen a television. Only twelve years later, he was on his way to becoming one of the most recognizable names and faces of the late twentieth century. Inspired by the success of the Beatles, Chaim gave up trying to make it in the conventional world, where he'd been an elementary school teacher and a typist at *Vogue,* among other occupations. He became Gene Klein and then Gene Simmons and started writing rock songs. When he picked up an electric bass, he showed a natural aptitude for the instrument, so much so that it's hard to understand why he's often slammed as a mediocre player. I've always maintained that to call him mediocre is to miss the entire point of Kiss. Anyway, whatever he does or doesn't do on the bass is deliberate; as part of my research for this assignment, I read a January '79 *Guitar Player* interview in which he spoke at great length about his style and equipment, and he was certainly as knowledgeable as any "credible" musician.

Prior to speaking with Simmons, I'd published just two feature-length articles, the first on John Taylor of Duran Duran and the second on Andy West of the Dixie Dregs. Both bassists had been friendly and cooperative, inviting me to their homes and giving me all the time I needed. When I called Mercury Records, I therefore assumed that the publicist would happily arrange for me to meet Simmons sometime in the following week. Instead, she instructed me to send a fax spelling out whether or not Gene would get the cover of the magazine. Then she hung up. Crushed, I spoke to *Bass Player* editor Jim

Roberts, who said he never made deals. Simmons would first have to give the interview, and only then would Jim decide if it deserved a cover. The story had been my idea, after all, and I still had tons of dues to pay.

With no hope whatsoever, I faxed my request to Mercury, explaining that the cover decision was out of my hands because I was only a tiny cog in a great machine. Two weeks passed. I gave it one last try and made a follow-up call, ready to do some serious begging. The publicist was almost gleefully vague, as if she thought I was hilarious, so I switched tactics and told her that I'd have to move on to another project since I could add nothing else to the discussion.

"Okay!" she trilled. "Thanks for the call! 'Bye!"

The matter seemed to have been resolved, but my phone rang a few days later, and someone who sounded a bit like the comedian Jackie Mason asked for "Tom Victor." I identified myself, and the caller boomed, "Gene Simmons! Whattaya got? What's the story? What's up?" Caught completely off guard, all I could come up with was "I would like to interview you," my voice pitched eerily high. "Well, let's *do* it," he said. "Right now." Since we both lived in Los Angeles, I didn't want to settle for a phone interview, so I suggested we meet. "Oh, are you one of *those?*" he groaned. "What is it with you face-to-face guys?" I started to explain that I could conduct a much more thorough interview if I spoke to him in person, but he cut me off, complaining, "It's just the bass. It's the *bass!* That's all it is!" He said he'd have to juggle his schedule and hung up.

The next day, he called in the afternoon and asked if I could meet him in half an hour. I told him I couldn't and wondered if he could give me more advance notice. *"Tom!"* he barked, "I'm a rock star! I'm being pulled in ten different directions at the same time. I . . . don't . . . *know* when I'll be available." I tried to point out that the inability to pin down a time was very unusual for me, that in the past my interview subjects had always—

He interrupted smoothly, saying, "Tom, you sound like a *really cool* guy, I'm sure, and I'm giving you more consideration than I give my own mother, but I just don't know. I'll call you back." *Click.*

The following morning, I canceled my appointments and sat in the breakfast nook next to the phone, starting at around eight. I had a pretty good novel and the radio, so I wasn't bored. Simmons called at 11:30 and we arranged to meet at 2:30 that afternoon at the Music Grinder Studio in Hollywood, where Kiss was recording their new album. I asked about bringing a photographer, but he said, "No. We're not going to take any pictures." I told him that a feature article with no photos would look pretty weird. After an indescribably awful pause, he hissed, "We'll figure all that out *later.* All right?" *Bam* went the phone, and I scurried off to pack my things.

To be on the safe side, I arrived at the studio half an hour early even though I expected an endless wait as Simmons turned the screws on me for making him do the interview in person. When I opened the front door, however, he was standing right inside, blocking my way and talking over his shoulder to someone behind him. I stared at the back of his head for what seemed like hours. When he finally turned around, his face had no expression at all. "I'm Gene," he said in a soft, absolutely neutral voice, his hand out. He's extremely tall and striking, even good-looking, despite his claim of being "the ugliest guy on the face of the planet." He also has the watchful stillness of a crocodile and the strangest, most disturbing eyes I've ever seen. It was impossible for me to guess what he was thinking.

He gave me two leaflets for his Gene Simmons Punisher Bass, stating, "*These* are for *you,*" and led me down a hallway to a lounge full of black leather-covered furniture. I sat in one of the chairs, and he used the wall rheostat to turn the lights down to a twilight murkiness. "That's much nicer, isn't it?" he commented as he arranged himself on the couch. Since he'd never specified how much time he was granting me, I asked if we could get started. "Oh sure," he said. "I'll talk your head off." I took my tape recorder out of my gym bag. "You know, you'd better give that to me," he murmured, so I numbly switched it on and surrendered it. He sat back and cradled it on his lap, his legs stretched out across the coffee table. He retained control of my recorder for most of the interview, gripping it tenderly with both hands as if it were a baby he was protecting. Along with our voices and the rustling of his leather pants, the tape picked up an electronic beeping that came from his watch or maybe another mechanism hidden somewhere under his clothes.

Okay. I've got it on all different authorities that you are a New Yorker; you are an Israeli, an ex-teacher, all sorts of things. I was wondering if you could just set the record straight, however you want.

I was born in the Holy Land, but every time people want to start a new religion based around me, like they did that other Jew, I tell them, "No, I'm doing fine. I'm making a great living. I don't mind paying taxes on the money I make." Whereas Jesus, or Yeshua ben Yoseph, as he was born, really figured it out. You start a religion, and then the money you make is tax free. Cool. It's a religion. I think I missed out. "Simmonsanity." Come on! It's got a sound to it.

So I come from there. I came here when I was nine. When I landed at La Guardia Airport—because at that point there was no Kennedy Airport; this was back when dinosaurs roamed the earth—there was a billboard showing Santa Claus smoking Kent cigarettes. And I had never seen Santa Claus, much less a Christian or a cross, coming from Israel, and I thought it was a rabbi smoking. He's got a beard, you know, a Russian rabbi because it's snowing outside and stuff. So there was massive culture shock.

And then when I discovered the Beatles, I was watching television. I must have been about twelve or thirteen. It changed me like no religious movement—or bowel movement, come to think of it—ever did. It single-handedly changed everything. Elvis [Presley] was a sex symbol and was important, but the Beatles changed the world. They changed fashion, hair length, clothes, opened the doors to free thinking beyond anything else.

They were the biggest force of music I can think of ever, that in the course of such a short time they completely changed the entire world to a different way of thinking. And they didn't mean to. They were just playing pop songs. And so after that I started singing in bands and originally picked up the guitar because I started writing songs right away, basically by ripping off Beatle chords and singing new verses and new lyrics to them. Then I looked around me and saw that everyone was playing guitar, so I switched to bass.

You said in an earlier interview for Guitar Player that there was something more male about the bass, as opposed to guitar.

Oh yeah. I mean it was just the harmonics. It may or may not be a sexist point of view, but I think there is such a thing as "balls," a male aggression chemically induced. Testosterone and all that. It simply exists. Feminists can talk all they want. Sorry, they do not have this chemical; they're out of luck. Bass played the right way can be a very, very aggressive instrument. It doesn't have to be a melodic instrument necessarily, although I've always tried to play melodies against the chords and tried not to use the bass ultimately as what it's always been used for, which is a rhythm instrument locked in with the kick and all that.

And I could give a shit. The kick means nothing to me. I'm much more interested sometimes . . . I mean, the line in the Beatles' "Michelle," for instance, should be played on a bass guitar. I think it was originally played on a fuzz guitar. But that's a bass line. [Sings melody from "Michelle."] There is a pulse to the overall piece, the musical piece, but the bass doesn't have to be that pulse. *All* the instruments can be adding a certain pulse.

I mean, we can't do this harmonically here, but if this is the pulse [snaps fingers rhythmically], the guitars are going *ah, ah, ah, ah, ah, ah,* and the bass is going *boom, bi-boom, boom bauhm boom boom doom,* the bass is certainly not keeping track of where the kick is or anything like that. But there is a pulse that the music is . . . All of it is inferring the pulse of the music. So I much prefer that. And then there's always drums.

So whenever we've played stuff, as primitive as it's always been and intended to be, I've tried not to just approach the bass as a sort of pumping, eighth-note instrument. That's more classically used in bands like AC/DC and other sorts of meat-and-potatoes bands that do it the best. There's already an AC/DC, so there's no reason to pump the bass. Been done. Been there, done that.

You said the day before yesterday something that I thought was very interesting. You said, "It's just the bass. It's just the **bass,** *" like it was something that doesn't merit any discussion. I don't know if you intended it to sound like—*

I didn't mean [grimaces] *"Just* the bass." I think the bass is the thing females react to the most sexually and males react to the most in terms of *heaviness.* They think it's a guitar, but they don't know. It's the bass. Without bass, you ain't got heavy. Take the bass out of the mix, and see how heavy the guitar is. It'll sound broken up and stuff. Without that low end, you got nothing. Balls, basically. You see a tall guy with little pea-sized balls, it's not the same thing. See a short guy with king-sized balls, now that's a *guy.*

That's a guy?

That's balls. And this is gonna make me a lot of friends, but fuck 'em all if they can't take a joke. And I mean that in a good way.

Okay. Uh, it seems that you've taken the time to craft your lines rather carefully.

A couple of guys very early on impressed me tremendously with how they completely ignored the kick drum: [Paul] McCartney, and way before him Felix Pappalardi [of Mountain] was great. Ron Wood was a terrific bass player in Jeff Beck's band. I'm not crazy about his guitar playing, but whatever was going on in those first two records, *Truth* and *The Beck Group,* that's as good as it gets, I think. I'm even much more of a fan of that kind of bass playing than I am of that on [Led] Zepp[elin] records, where you can't hear the bass. It's so round, it's just like a shadow that goes by. I want to hear the notes, which is why I like to use a pick. I like picks in my hand. I want to hear those notes. If you're going to play something where you'll just feel, fuck that. I wanna feel it, and I wanna *hear* it go by.

You know, there's the R & B point of view which is used in the old R & B tunes, the old Motown thing. You sort of felt the bass moving around, but you didn't know what it was. And then finally hip-hop and all that stuff took the balls by the horns [pauses and looks over to make sure I got his pun] and decided to almost completely get rid of every other instrument *except* the bass. The bass became the backbone, and the guitar was just reduced to *pink-pinka-chink,* just picking in the background. They're not even playing chords. And the bass is all. And that's the basis of hip-hop and black music today. The bass movement. Synth bass, unfortunately, but . . .

How do you feel about synth bass?

I'm not a fan of it. I don't . . . Electronics by and large have turned out to be . . . When electronics are the master, it becomes cold and inhuman to me. When *we* control the electronics, I find it very refreshing. When you push a machine past the point where it's supposed to go, some of the industrial stuff I think is terrific. Some of what Trent Reznor and Flood [British producer Mark Ellis] have done on those records is a lot of fun. A lot of exciting stuff. And yet people have been there before.

There've been those early [modern-music composer Karl-heinz] Stockhausen pieces. Very, very dissonant. A lot of sort of almost postimpressionistic sonic artists who played around with sound and what it means and messed with sound structure. Somewhere in there, between pop-song structure and industrial sonics, is Nine Inch Nails, where it finally connects with people. Songs you like with a lot of cool-sounding stuff. But certainly the instruments are used "incorrectly" in the sense that an engineer will say, "Well, you're pinning the needles! That's not good!" The engineer's wrong; the artist is right. It *is* good. It's better to pin the instruments.

Don't limit your music by limiting the instrument you're playing on. A fine craftsman is never going to blame his tools. In

---

OVERLEAF— *Kiss, from left: Gene Simmons, Peter Criss, Paul Stanley, and Ace Frehley*

essence, a craftsman is not going to say, "I can't play this because the instrument's not designed for it." Fuck that! You know? Change the tuning. Break it apart. I mean, it's great to hear Presidents of the United States [of America] coming out. The bass player [Chris Ballew]'s got two strings. Cool. Cool! Who said it's gotta have four? While other bass players are going eight, twelve, sixteen, a million strings, go down to two.

Why haven't you gone to a five-, six-, or eight-string bass?

Why?

To get even more "balls," as you put it.

It's unnecessary. There's nothing like a battleship that's got so much armament that it sinks under the weight of its own guns. You've gotta be . . . I mean, walk in there with the proper armament, be ready for battle, but be able to move around. A lumbering hulk is just . . . You know, the machines that you get . . .

I mean, it's like your video machine at home. It's got so many fucking buttons. You tell me if you've figured out what that flashing 12:00 sign means. Nobody knows how to work that thing. It is the most irritating thing. More black tape has been sold just to cover up that flashing light that tells you the time. Nobody knows how to set it because it's unnecessary. That's why I think that in certain kinds of music, the backbone of rock and roll, whether you call it mainstream or not, it's still rock and roll. It's still guitar, drums, bass, and if it's that, I got news for you: It's still rock and roll.

That's why digital just has not worked. Whether you take a Dinosaur Junior record, a Smashing Pumpkins record, it ain't digital. And if it *is* digital, you've gotta punish the recording instrument so that it succumbs to human will. Because ultimately it's about human will and not mechanical stuff. That's my biggest bone with R & B that's machine based. You punch up a couple numbers, it gives you the beats per second, and there's your drumbeat. It's computer music. I don't buy it. And that's why the artist is never important and why they never last more than an album or two, and that's why there are no catalog sales on hip-hop or R & B. There are some terrific grooves on there, but it's form over substance. You'll dance to it, and you'll ask the people on the dance floor, "Who is that?" and they'll say, "I don't know, but I love their song 'Pump It Up, Baby,' or whatever it's called."

Is this one of the reasons you've been around as a band as long as you have?

You know, I don't have a fuckin' clue. It's a mystery to me. Kiss fans are beyond anything.

Are they still known as the Kiss Army?

Yeah, that's what they call themselves. We didn't start it. It started in Terre Haute, Indiana, when a radio station didn't want to play Kiss. A guy named Bill Starkey—not related to Ringo [Starr]—kept calling to have Kiss records played, and the DJ said, "That's not our philosophy. We don't do that." So Starkey said, "You'd *better* do that because by five o'clock, when everybody gets out of school, we're gonna surround your beacon with the Kiss Army." The DJ just ignored it. At five o'clock, they called the cops and everything, and there was a helicopter that showed thousands surrounding this thing.

This is real?

Oh, this is real. It made the front page of the Terre Haute newspaper. I have the newspaper. It said, KISS ARMY INVADES RADIO STATION, and the Kiss Army was born. And from then on, it's been self-run. If it's an army, it certainly isn't a conscripted army. They're all volunteers, and if you check the Internet, they have their own web sites; they talk amongst themselves; they buy, sell, trade. It's beyond belief. Go to any collectors' show, and you'll see Elvis, Kiss, and the Beatles memorabilia in that order. And he's dead.

Does this put a heavy responsibility on your shoulders?

None. None. If anybody's looking to me as a sort of leader, they're fooling themselves, 'cause I'm a complete buffoon. I enjoy being one, and nobody does it better, James Bond notwithstanding. [Hums theme song from film *The Spy Who Loved Me*.]

Chapter Two

Self-Defense, Girls, and God

I'd like to tell you something about the reactions I got from people when I told them I'd be doing this interview.

[Holds up hand.] May I cut you off? Thank you. First of all, depending on the age and whether it's a male or a female, the reaction was totally different. To older females, a joke, not real. To males in their thirties, gods: "I grew up with them; they're the best." It's never gray. It's always love or hate. And I would have it no other way.

Why?

Because life should be that way. Anything that's so-so . . . Apathy is death. It's the black-and-whites that make everything possible. Hot and cold. Who cares about lukewarm? It ain't hot; it ain't cold. "How's the movie?" [Shakes head.] "Ehh, all right."

Dovetailing into that, it seems your later material is a lot more hostile than the earlier songs, when you were singing about "100,000 Years" [Kiss], "Cold Gin" [Kiss], and then on the latest album [Revenge], we have more aggressive songs like "Spit." Is this deliberate?

Not really. I think everybody sits down, whether they're a painter, a writer, or whoever, and puts stuff down that's going on. Not that we're reporters of modern culture as we know it, and yet when we sit down and write a song, whether it's conscious or unconscious, we're putting down stuff that we feel comfortable with. So the song I write today is not the same song I would have written twenty-three years ago, which was when we started. Nor do I look exactly the same as I did twenty-three years ago. In other words, *How Can You Be in Two Places at Once When You're Not Anywhere at All?* (Firesign Theatre, Columbia Records.)

I'm not sure I could write the same song I did then today, and I sure as hell would not have been able, back then, to write the songs that I write today. If there's a connection and it fits—and that record [points to my copy of *Revenge*] is about four years old—but if there's a connection and it fits, then hopefully it's not the exact same thing. I don't want to do the exact same thing. Again, we're still within the confines of electric guitar, bass, and drums; and although the form is very limiting, you still somehow want to move on and not keep writing the same songs.

So lyrically I'm sure there's a difference. There's even some stuff here [points thumb over his shoulder to studio] that I'm sure is very aggressive. This record that we're finishing up in about a week is the studio record, and that's going to be out after the *Unplugged* album. So in March we have the MTV or whatever, Kiss *Unplugged* record, with a long-playing video. Along with it is going to be a ten-dollar magazine called *Kiss Nation,* which is going to have a fifty-page comic book *Kiss Meets the X-Men,* written by Stan Lee, where we hang out with Doctor Strange, Spider-Man, all the cool guys, and the X-Men. The rest of the magazine is Kiss articles by fans, and so on. Perfect bound like the *Playboy* magazine size, with a pullout poster that comes out at the same time. And this album is not going to come out for a while. And it's even more aggressive. There's a song on it called "Hate." [Sings part of song.]

And you believe that [humans are full of hate]?

Yeah. I think once you . . . When you're innocent, young, and naïve, you perceive—I did—a different world. The more you live and the more you learn, certain realities become apparent. Like when you're a kid, and you live in your mom's house, you never think of locking the doors. Somebody else does that for you. Or earning money, or whatever. Nowadays, you're wearing condoms, locking the doors, squeezing your butt tight because at any point somebody's gonna fuck you without your consent. The nature of mankind—I don't like to get heavy here—the nature of mankind is not what we've been taught. I think there's an inherently evil and very present side, and our canine teeth are not accidents. They're designed that way. Testosterone is not an accident. We have not only the ability but the instinct to kill. Pecking orders and all that stuff. We have to work at becoming good because it's too easy to become evil. It's inherent in all of us, from siblings just torturing each other, from bullies in school just for the joy of it, just because "I'm stronger than you. I'm going to pick on you." No different than animals. The more beautiful a girl is, the more she wants the ugly girl to feel unattractive. It's complete and utter tyranny. In conversations, the bright person's going to make the person who's not so bright feel like a complete dolt because he wants to feel superior. I'm as guilty of that as anybody.

Well, if you're aware of all this, why not junk it?
Because it's easier said than done. If somebody cuts you off on the highway when you're driving, the first words that come out, you know— Your blood boils. You have to fight it, count to ten, and so on. Culture and civilization supposedly fight that, but the instinct gets there first. The fight to be good is the continuing fight. It's not the other way around. It's not like, "I'm feeling happy and good, and I love everybody. Feel the love in the air. I want to get angry so I'm going to work at getting angry." No, it's the other way around. Instinctively, we want to kill. We have to fight that urge. *That's* what "Hate" is about.

Okay. I was going to say earlier—
What an article for a bass magazine.
Well, I'll use it wherever I can. We'll see what happens.
Really.
So there were two universal reactions people had when I told them I was going to do this interview. Everybody either said, "Gene Simmons?! The Gene Simmons?" or

*they said, "Be careful. Watch out." Without exception. So
after everything you've just spoken about—*

I like both reactions.

*Why? I mean, you're a grown man. Why do you need to
intimidate and instill uneasiness?*

I want to be feared because it's one of the few ways that you
can be safer. Because meekness invites disaster. The beautiful
idea of religion, that the meek shall inherit the earth, is naïveté
at its highest. It's a beautifully romantic idea. Without God, the
meek inherit shit. The meek inherit squat. The strong inherit the
earth. It's the law of nature. I've never been in a fight in my life.
Not one. Not even in school, and I've also never picked on anybody. But I prefer to be looked at as a dark figure who could
potentially kick your ass or slit your throat or whatever, even
though I won't. It's only a wonderful armor, so nobody bothers
me. It's like— Some of the animals in the rainforest are very
fierce looking. They look poisonous. Something like a Gila mon-
ster, or some of the snakes, look very poisonous so that other
animals won't bother them. They'll run away. But these snakes
bother nobody. So the girls are right. I'm a snake. You're right.

Okay. Can we talk about—

Shit, if I'd have been in the Garden of Eden, I'd have given Eve
the apple too.

Why?

Well, 'cause I don't have to take her out for a full dinner. She'll
put out just for an apple; *bam,* I'm in. Adam's away, Eve's gonna
play.

*Now you're doing it again. After all that sensitivity, this
crude intimidation stuff.*

Fuck yeah. Because it's so much more fun to be a bad boy
without *actually* being a bad boy than it is being an angel.
Because then there's nothing to talk about.

*So can we talk about sexism then? Charges that a lot of
your work is misogynistic?*

It is.

There are lots of female bassists who read the magazine—

They're right. Without question, they're completely right. It's hairy gorilla music; they're right. But I think their anger is a little misguided because the entire genre is by definition sexist. So if I'm in the genre, don't pick on me for being true to its manifesto. Because rock and roll, the definition is cock and balls. It is men's music. Women want to play it, great. But they haven't succeeded yet. *Rock and roll,* I'm talking about. Spread your legs; bang your guitar. Okay, so you have Melissa Etheridge, but you still need guys in back of her.

Every band is filled with guys. I don't see any girl bands. One or two come and go. See ya, 'bye! It ain't serious. It's pop stuff. Not that it's no . . . You know, girls are going to complain [shouts in falsetto], *"I can do anything you can do!"* It's not true. I can lift twice as much as you can. End of story. I don't wanna hear a discussion. *"I can run as fast as you can!"* You can't! I can outrun you. I'm designed that way. *"Well, if I hit you I can hurt you!"* You're wrong. If I hit you once in the jaw, you're dead. That doesn't mean that women are not much more intelligent or capable of feeling more pain or anything; but physically, there's just no way.

I'll sing lower than you. I'll lift heavier things, so if rock and roll is about sort of aggressive vocal prowess and sounding like a bull—as opposed to a bullshitter, though I'm a little of both—cows don't sound like bulls. Sorry! This is bull music. The very phrase "rock and roll" comes from old black musicians down in Mississippi and means [shouts] "FUCK!" The actual definition of "rock and roll" is fucking. "Let me rock and roll you all night long." Guess what he's talking about? So if they're accusing me of being sexist, I say "Thank you" because that's being true to the form. "Gene Simmons is too politically incorrect." Guess what? It ain't rock and roll.

So again, just to—

But I tell you what: The very same girl that's gonna say, "That guy's such a sexist pig," she knows secretly in her heart that I'm gonna be a much better fuck than that guy who can quote [Friedrich] Nietzsche and [Søren] Kierkegaard to her. Even though I read the same books, that's not what I'm about. That's not my calling card. "Look! I'm well educated! I smoke a pipe!" Well, fuck *you*. I'll fuck your pants off. The *girls,* that is. It's not my fault. I'm designed that way. [Sings from the Hassles' "Every Step I Take (Every Move I Make)."]

["Every Breath You Take"?]

No, that's [the Police]. [Continues humming for a few seconds.] The Hassles. *That's* where that comes from. Billy Joel. That's where that comes from. Long Island band. On, ah . . .

Well, I was just going to ask, where does it end?

When you're finally in the ground. When you're six feet under. It's not my fault! I mean, every old prick who's got a glass of water near his bed with his teeth floating in it still looks at the nurse and wants to jump her bones. Even if his dick doesn't work. He has no choice. Mentally, he's still out there.

So, to the person that says, "That's soooo juvenile!" you answer . . .

Well, I think I'm much more in touch with myself. A little more honest, perhaps. The same person that says it's juvenile is wankin' in the bathroom with a *Playboy* foldout or whatever. They can't help it! And if they refuse to touch their pecker, their body naturally builds up that semen and starts to ejaculate all by itself in their sleep. Sorry! You got any problems with the design, talk to the woman up there, 'cause it ain't a man. 'Cause you know God is a woman.

No, I don't.

Oh, absolutely! I'll prove it to you. [Returns to strident falsetto.] *"You will have no other god before me because if you so much as look at another god, I'll have to—"* What is *that,* if it's not a jealous bitch? If God is so all-powerful, why would you care if I prayed to another god? What's the matter, your ego is fragile? You can't take me praying to another god? That is a *woman.* "We are all children of God." What kind of image does that bring to mind? A father or a mother? [Long pause.]

Mother.

The defense rests; next case. So we've covered religion, testosterone . . .

So let's get back to songwriting. You've said you—

All this stuff, incidentally, goes into songwriting, if you're honest enough with yourself. And I don't think I'm a great songwriter. The fact that tons of people cover this stuff every year is great. I don't really place myself or anyone in the band in the Lennon–McCartney world. *That's* beyond. *That's* perfect songwriting.

[Kiss guitarist-vocalist Paul Stanley wanders into lounge.]
Simmons: [Points to Stanley.] *That's* Paul Stanley.
Hi, Paul Stanley.
Stanley: Hi.
Simmons: *Bass* magazine.
Tom Wictor. **Bass** PLAYER *magazine.*
Stanley: Hi, Tom.
Simmons: [To Stanley.] There's not an ounce of fat on that stuff.
Nice to see you. **[Shaking hands with Paul Stanley.]** *We're talking about religion and testosterone.*
Simmons: [Referring to Stanley.] He's never heard this before. He's never heard me give a damn interview before.
Stanley: After I taught Gene the fundamentals of bass, he developed his own approach.
[Stanley leaves.]

That's what I figured.
Yeah.
Really?
Yup. The basics.
So you were the original—
No, he's pulling your wanker.
I know he's pulling my wanker. What I'm asking is, You were the original two members?
That's right.
So how long have you known each other?
Oh, longer than any band has a right to exist. What we feel

like is the two idiots in, what was that [film], *Bill and Ted's Excellent Adventure.* The Grim Reaper comes to claim them, and they hoodwink the guy, and the guy says, "All right, I give up." So they get to live their lives over and over again. That's what we feel like, Bill and Ted. Are we as stupid? You bet. Beavis and Butt-head? Oh, much, *much* stupider than that. But we will outlast you and your kind. We are the cockroaches that will inherit the earth. Revile us; hate us; after you're long gone, we'll still be here.

You said you cover this stuff every interview. Is that true? I've never seen it.

I basically say what I feel. I'm the same guy, although everything gets edited. I mean, if you're talking to a guitar magazine, and I start spouting my views on life, death, and the male species as we know it, most magazines—*Hit Parade* or some such rag—won't print that.

This isn't Hit Parade. You'll be surprised how much will get in.

I understand. I understand. [Pause.] I think it's *really wonderful* that women take up bass playing and men take up knitting. Terrific.

But?

One or the other is not going to be really good at it. Incidentally, the way we're designed, for some reason our abilities with our fingers is nowhere near as developed as it is in females.

Yeah, I've heard that.

Much more tactile. So they're better at cutting diamonds, so they can wear more of them, and they're sure better at knitting. We're not designed as well as you are for knitting. It's not my fault, so don't hurt me for that. And wielding the heaviest of stringed instruments, the bass? We're designed to carry it better.

But you've been playing a relatively small bass for years, haven't you?

It's *medium*-sized. The Gene Simmons Punisher is my own design. I sell it myself. If you want one, you can call 1-609-

PUNISHER. It costs fifteen hundred bucks. Each one is signed. Each one is handmade.

I'll bet they don't come in left-handed models, do they?

Absolutely not. Remember, the left is the sign of the Devil. South*paw,* not even south-*hand.* You didn't know that? Oh, absolutely. Sure.

You'd think that that would appeal to the protective image you were talking about earlier. I mean, the skull rings you wear and all that.

I don't see skulls as being sinister at all. We all have one underneath our skins. It's what you see, selective perception and all that, the reality of the beholder. I mean, I see you, and I see skin and all that, but underneath it I see a grinning skull.

Yeah, but soldiers have worn skull emblems on their helmets to inspire—

Fear. Yeah, well, when *you* see a cross, you see a religious, beautiful thing. When *I* see it, I see it as a sign of torture. Like if Christ were killed today, there'd be many millions of people running around with little electric chairs hanging around their necks, or little guns. You know, here's a religious symbol that's a sign of torture. Jewish torture. I find when I look at a cross, I don't find it beautiful at all. I find the ideal behind it beautiful, but I find the cross the most macabre, bloodthirsty . . . Blood. You know, "Here, eat my body; drink my blood." *What?!* If that ain't cannibalism, I don't know what is. Of course now we've got the feminists, anybody who's religious coming after me. But hey . . . [Shrugs.]

It's gonna be great.

But don't touch me. I'm one of the Chosen. Touch me, and I'm gonna tell Jesus. He's one of our guys too.

What about this? [I show him *Revenge* CD, covering "KI" in Kiss logo so that only "SS" shows; result looks exactly like lightning-bolt symbol of Nazi SS in World War Two.]

[Entire demeanor changes; becomes very serious.] You know, people have told us from day one about the SS. Just for the record, I'm Israeli, Jewish. I was born that way; it's not even a choice. It's who I am. My mother was in a concentration camp. Paul is Jewish. We'd be the last people on the face of the planet to even fool around with that stuff. I wanted to call the new album *Chamber Music. (Something) Chamber Music.* You know, like it was a vault, and I couldn't think of another word. Paul said, "How about *Gas Chamber Music?*" And immediately we both went, "Wait a minute." He meant like the music you hear when you're being executed. There used to be these guys who'd play music as you were being electrocuted.

Really?

Yes! As people were being hung, they'd get a string quartet. It was, you know, death chamber music. And when Paul said *Gas Chamber Music,* all of us reacted. We said we're not going to use that because it's too insensitive to what went on in World War Two. It's beyond insensitive. And if you think the people who did that were insane, incidentally, just to speak on history, you yourself are out of your fuckin' mind. You're as insane as you think they are. That's a choice. The potential for evil in the human mind is endless.

I'm part German, so I know all about it.

Well, it's endless. The inventive cruelty of man to man is beyond anything. Animals kill, eat, and that's it. *We* torture. That's beyond.

Well, then, I have to ask again about your image. I know it's for safety's sake, but why not—

Look: You're going through a black neighborhood— And don't give me this liberal, politically correct bullshit about "We're all brothers." Fuck yourself. You're going through a black neighborhood, your life's in danger, period. I don't care how you got there. "My ancestors were slaves." Go fuck yourself. You're going through a black neighborhood, you're gonna die. How are you gonna appear to everybody? Meek? Or strong, like you can kick their ass back? You have a choice. Life is a black neighborhood. End of story. Whether you're black or white. If you're black, and you're in a black neighborhood, you better walk the walk and talk the talk. The reason everybody there sounds like

they're completely mongoloid is because if you're literate, it sounds weak. So it's better to say, "Yo, man," and it's better to say "motherfucker" because you come off like a badass, and so you can survive another day. There is no choice.

But do you have that many enemies, for lack of a better term? Is it really that necessary?

I think from the moment you wake up in the morning you've got enemies surrounding you, whether someone physically assaults you or just goes after your pocketbook. Or you get married, and then your wife divorces you, and one of your two God-given balls walks out in her purse as she leaves. How did she get half of what you've got? Why don't *you* get half of what *she's* got? Or you wake up, and the government decides to take almost 50 percent of what you make out the door. Or you order a plumber to come in and fix your stuff, and he sees you live in a good neighborhood and charges you double. What's the difference if it's economic cruelty, mental cruelty, or physical cruelty?

So are you always on guard, expecting the worst?

When you cross the street, do you look both ways?

Yeah.

Why? Don't you trust people? Do you think they're gonna run you down if you don't look at them?

But when I'm sitting in my living room I don't look under the sofa or under the chairs.

Neither do I. But is the door locked in your house?

It is.

It is in mine too. Gee, you're just like me. What's the matter, don't you want to leave the door open?

[Pause.] Well—

Answer the question! [Sits forward and flaps hand in my face.] See, when you ask me questions, I answer. When *I* ask *you,* you change the subject.

[Pause.] You're being rhetorical, though.

I'm not retorted. [Laughs.]

You're being rhetorical. You're messing with me.

No, I'm not. I'm making a very clear point. It's all about perception.

It is?

You're looking at the desert, and you see palm trees and all that, and I'm saying, "No, it's not there. I don't care what you see. We're in a desert. It makes no sense." What's out there is bleak. I'm seeing through the mirage. You love the mirage; it's okay! We're both walking through the same desert. The same laws of gravity affect both of us, even though you, in your fantasy world—meaning "you" as somebody out there—just see the mirage. That's okay! It's cool. It's beautiful; it's got water and palm trees. I may *see* the mirage. I may *hope for* the mirage. I *know* it's not there. So I guard myself. I don't drink all my water; I take little sips, and I save.

Don't you think we need a little fantasy to keep from going insane, though?

Sure. Kiss. That's why when I get up on stage, I don't wanna go, "Here's who I really am." Fuck that.

Is that because it's dangerous or because it's just not what you're into?

Well, what's the Thing in the Fantastic Four, dangerous or a superhero? What's the [Incredible] Hulk? Scary or not? That's real stuff to me. Superman is really the *Übermensch,* the bastardized version of what Nietzsche used because Nietzsche's writings didn't support that at all. It was his sister who completely distorted his teachings so that the Nazis got ahold of them and changed them. That's white, Anglo-Saxon, Protestant fantasy. The Great White Hope. That's the fantasy. The reason Marvel superheroes finally connected with everybody is because they showed dangerous, mixed-up people, and people reacted to them and said, "That's real. That's real." Spider-Man. Scary-looking guy. Cops don't like him; robbers don't like him; he's an outcast, and he's got problems with his girl. He has an identity crisis and self-esteem problems. People. [Sings from Bob Merrill and Jule Styne's "People."]

I think the world's a pretty bleak place, and you have a choice of crossing the street and not looking and believing in man's kindness to man, that nobody will run you over. I choose to think that there's a good chance somebody will. However, if I'm in the car, I will not run somebody over. As proof of that, I've never picked a fight with anybody. You know, once or twice you head-butt somebody to get them out of the way, but pick on no one and also look bad so that nobody picks on you. What other choice have you got? [Long pause as he looks at me, clearly waiting for answer. Not wanting to get yelled at again, I comply.]

Chapter Three

Shut Up and Talk

Okay. I actually think about that a lot, but I'm not the sort of person who can really comment on it because I tend to be something of a natural target.

There's no such fuckin' thing.

There is.

I'll prove it to you: The most powerful, history-changing people have been little wimps. End of story.

Yeah, okay, but I don't mean physically, but whatever it is that we give off, that pheromone or whatever it is.

No, it starts with physicality. Once you get the point physically across, self-esteem and how you come across is all first impression. First impression: how you dress, what you say, where you are. Very few people get a chance to see beyond that stuff.

No. Do you really think so? That's it?

You see a stripper on stage, or a Republican on the platform, or an actor, or a beautiful girl with big tits, immediately your mind takes over. She's got big tits; they're a little exposed; she's easy. She could be a fuckin' nun. But because you can see a little flesh on her heaving breasts, you think, "Oh, she's showing 'em because she wants me to go over there." See a guy with glasses and a pipe, you think you can kick his ass, even though it's not necessarily so. See a guy with shades on—without the pipe—and whatever the signs of strength are, that tells you something.

Here, I'm gonna make a sign for you. Ready? [Gives patented Gene Simmons scowl.] This is what? Oh, anger. [Gives horribly goofy grin; speaks in dorky voice.] "Hello! Hello!" What do you make out of that? [Long pause.]

Well . . . One is anger; one is . . . not-anger?

Well, one is "Don't mess with me"; the other is a buffoon. "I can take you. Wanna buy a bridge?"

I wish I wasn't writing for a bass magazine because I'd love to take you on on that one.

[Laughs.] No chance. I mean, there's no hope.

Okay. I'd composed a letter I was going to write to my editor, saying, "Mr. Simmons doesn't have time to do the interview, based on the phone conversations we've had."

I don't do chitchat stuff. You know, I started hearing your life story. What, when, where, how. See?

No.

I mean, when you started talking on the phone, I started to get the impression you were sitting back, getting comfortable, ready to have a conversation. I'm going, "Just give me when you're available. If you're not, *boom*. [Mimes slamming down telephone.] I'll get back to you." Life's short. Gotta move on.

Sure. Yeah. Okay. It is, in that sense. But I'd never experienced such a, a brusque way of doing business. It doesn't inspire—

People to like me?

No, it's not a question of liking or disliking. I just figured that the interview was down the crapper, so I was already composing the letter to my editor letting him know.

Good.

Good? Why good?

Don't be too available. Girls know this better than guys.

Yeah, but I don't want to marry you; I just wanted to get an interview.

Same thing. It's all perception. Perception is all. Before first impression. And the reality is I don't have time for that stuff. This is *my* life. [Pulls out and shows me his date book; every line is filled with names, dates, and phone numbers.] I mean, I don't have time for that stuff. You know, you're in here as one thing, but you know, I don't have time! I mean, life to me is—you've got the mallet in the funhouse—you've got those beavers sticking their heads up and down in the holes, and you go *pow-pow-pow!* Try to hit as many as you can. And that's it.

Doesn't it get lonely, though?

It's the best! Don't believe the idea of success and power being lonely. You can have anyone, at any time, for any reason. On any level.

If that's what you're into. But what if you're not into that? What if you're into other things?

Then don't be a rock star. Go live on a mountaintop and be a hermit. Look at trees. That's valid. Not for me, though. I'd hang myself.

So you were a teacher, weren't you?

Short time. Spanish Harlem. Sixth grade. How about we take a break?

[We stop, and Simmons leaves for a few minutes. When he comes back, he receives a call on the phone in the corner. "Yes. No. Bring her over," he snaps and hangs up. He turns and stares at me with an indecipherable expression. "Come here a second," he says softly. "I want to show you something." His manner has become ultragentle, a remarkably ominous change; he seems totally evil now. I ask him not to hurt me, to which he replies, "No, no. Just come over here. Come on." He tilts his head to the side and beckons with his fingers. "*Come* on," he coaxes, almost whistling for me. I get up and walk over to him, expecting the worst. He points to a wall photo of a blond, breast-implanted, lip-enhanced, L.A.–generic woman with heavy makeup. "What do you think of her?" he asks. I snort and shake my head. Simmons, who's towering over me like a gallows, only eight inches away, mimics my snort.

"'Phh'? What does that mean?" he murmurs, inspecting me. I tell him I don't know. "Well, what do you think of her?" he insists. "Tell me. What are the first words that come to mind when you look at her?" I capitulate and come up with descriptions like *nothing special, uninteresting, a dime a dozen.* I ask him if he knows this person or something, if he's setting me up. I'm afraid he's suddenly going to scream, "Well, that's my *wife!*" Instead, he smiles faintly and croons, "No, no. Not at all. Keep going." I babble out a few more unflattering adjectives and trail off. He continues gazing at me and then taps the photo lightly with his index finger, saying, "Maybe. But I could have her if I wanted." He waits for a reaction, so I tell him that that's great. He nods and whispers, "It is."

After a moment of quiet reflection, he asks, "So you really wouldn't want someone like her?" I tell him no. "Well," he presses, "what sort of woman are you attracted to?" I'm confused, having just been told that he *didn't* want to hear all about me. "GILLIAN ANDERSON," I shout, the only famous name I can remember. He turns from the photo and glowers, demanding, "Who?" I explain that she's the FBI agent in the television show *The X-Files.* He looks away, nodding. "Oh, right. Sure. I can see that. Well, she can come to the party too."

Me, Gene, the blond, and Gillian. With this ghastly image ricocheting around the inside of my head, we sit back down to continue the interview, staying on the subject of rock stars.]

To hear any white, middle-class, upper-class, or even lower-class white person talk about problems, I don't *wanna* hear it. The entire white, sort of self-destructive thing is so rampant in today's music. Musically, it's such an exciting period, you know. But the heart of it is so full of bullshit and posing. I can just imagine [Pearl Jam's] Eddie Vedder saying to himself, "Fuck! Kurt Cobain killed himself, now I can't do that. He beat me to the punch. What's left for me to do?" It's such bullshit! I mean, the idea's to *win!* There's no choice!

You don't think that smacks a little of amorality?

No. I'll tell you why: because given half the chance, the bad guys don't play by the same rules, unfortunately. And democracy I don't think works. It just doesn't.

What are you talking about here, totalitarianism?

Yes. An enlightened, benevolent monarchy is absolutely the perfect form of government. The problem is [that] the people should have the power. When the monarchy isn't working, when this guy isn't working, kill him. Or get him out of the way, in jail, whatever. But too many chiefs . . . You wanna talk about making a straight line or a curved line down a highway, it goes to Congress, and two years later they're still talking about it. It don't work.

I had an image last night of the Kiss Army rising up and sweeping you into office. Do you have any political ambitions?

No, because I believe in the Machiavellian concept of power corrupting. I believe that, if you get in there, to survive, you have to start playing the game. Talking the talk and walking the walk. It dilutes and robs you. Guys like [Steve] Forbes, who I may or may not agree with politically, comes like a breath of fresh air. Because here's a guy who I think is not going to need the money. I want the president to have five hundred million dollars or more. I want this. I want it because if somebody comes to him and says, "Write a book for a million dollars," he won't say, "Yeah!" I want the richest man in the world to be president. You bet.

Doesn't your own position give you lots of power?
I have enormous power.

Well, are you corrupted?
Absolutely!

Doesn't that bother you?
No, because I hold it in check. But I'm fully aware that I'm spoiled, corrupted, but hopefully sane. And like all insane urges we have, if we're sane we control them. Look: Every day of the week, you, I, all of us, wake up in the morning and crave the stupidest, worst things we could possibly eat. That's what we wanna eat. Tell me you're not corrupted. As a child, you start being spoon-fed sugar. It corrupts you! You become addicted to it. You like it. You know full well it's bad for you. And it's a daily fight, like alcoholism or whatever. It's a daily fight not to eat the bad stuff. Sure I'm corrupted. But I fight it. I know I'm spoiled. I know I have too much money. I fuck way too much, especially for somebody my age. I should be sixteen or eighteen. Guys in their forties don't get as much puss. That's the French word, *pussé. Pussé voulez,* not the vulgar American term.

No, of course not.
But my cup *way* runneth over. Much more than people on the street. And so that—because stuff comes easy—corrupts. And if it corrupts you, you become spoiled.

So you're not a follower of the idea that at a certain point you try to get beyond all that?
Well, you're either an Epicurean hedonist, which is the pursuit of pleasure for pleasure's sake . . . If you buy that, then that brings happiness. Abstinence does not, in certain circum-

stances, make the heart grow fonder. Starving is not my cup of tea.

But hedonism is?

The pursuit of pleasure? I know very few sane people who don't want pleasure. And then it's only relative.

It's relative, okay.

Oh yeah. You can only handle one glass of water; I may be able to handle two. Which one of us is corrupt? It's all relative.

So is any pleasure the same as hedonism, in your book? Can there be such a thing as too much pleasure?

It's all relative. Too much for whom, you or I?

For you.

There's no absolute. Too much pleasure? You bet. Tickling is fun. Tie me up and don't let me pull my foot away, though, and I'll go insane.

[Paul Stanley walks into lounge again.]

Stanley: See ya.

Simmons: What? Whaat? Whaaaaat?

Stanley: Nothing to do.

Simmons: What'd we do with the solo?

Stanley: Finishing with the guitar and then going on to some other tunes.

Simmons: Why not this?

Stanley: He doesn't wanna hear it anymore.

Simmons: Ah. [Pause.] Well? Any parting words?

Stanley: [To me.] Go in peace.

Thank you very much.

Simmons: [Laughs loudly.]

Stanley: Talk to you later.

Simmons: [Calls after Stanley, who has walked out of lounge.] Are you going to Green Jelly? You don't have to go today, but I'm gonna—

Stanley: [From hallway.] I'd much rather get something done. You know, they got like a little bit done, and if he's got an idea, I'd rather realize it a little more.

Simmons: [To me.] Hold on a second.
Sure.

[The tape recorder is turned off while they talk animatedly around the corner. I strain to eavesdrop at first but decide I'd better not. I sit on the floor next to the coffee table because the deep chair is killing my back. Simmons returns and sits on the sofa, pointing to the two leaflets for his Punisher Bass that lie on the table next to my recorder.]

I don't know if you can take that and reproduce it or do something with it so you can have something to look at. Because I want to push that.
Yeah. Sure. Absolutely.
It's mail order, not really available through stores.
What they'll do is have an equipment sidebar which—
Fuck that. Nobody reads those.
No way! Everyone reads those!
COME ON! [Laughs derisively.]
You wouldn't believe the fanatics who read this magazine.
Nobody gives a shit. If it's got an interview, they'll read it. That's all. There are very few technoheads, very few. When you say "*Every*body . . . " [Shrugs.]
The ones who buy the magazine . . . I mean, have you ever even seen the magazine?
Sure. When you've had somebody famous on the cover, I've looked at it. When it's nobody I've ever heard of in a jazz band, I don't. It's the stars that pull it, not the bass.
Well, for you, maybe, but—
The masses. People.
It's for bass players. Bass players buy the magazine. They want to know this stuff. If we don't give them this stuff—
Well, I wanna make the point that if you have a famous bass player, then people who don't play the bass will buy it because they're interested in the person. Because it's not the bass; it's the person who plays the bass that makes it interesting.

OPPOSITE— *Gene Simmons (left), and a friend*

Absolutely. But they do well with their jazz players on the cover. I mean, the magazine went from being a one-off to being a monthly magazine. It's still growing, so—

The way to grow and become big? Stars. There's no choice. It's not even if I like it or not.

Weellll— I don't buy that.

You have a bass guitar on the cover, and there's no person in back of it, you won't sell as many. Sorry.

Yeah, it's true, but—

But that was my point, only. The fame of the person playing the bass will probably coincide with higher numbers. More. Movies. Food. Commercials.

Okay! Yes! You're right!

Okay! [Sits forward, eager.]

Okay, I'd like to—

Where did you grow up? Berkeley or someplace?

No. Venezuela. I'm a Venezuelan by birth.

¿Habla español?

Sí. Pero estoy olvidando mí español. Why?

I'm testing you.

You're testing me? No, no. I mean, why do you want to know where I'm from?

Because the American quick glance at somebody Hispanic or Latin . . . That word "Latin" is bullshit because nobody speaks Latin, get the fuck outta here. Spanish is not European. But I know Argentina, and I know that a lot of the racial stock is Italian and German.

The "quick glance"? I don't know what you mean. Were you trying to figure me out from physical appearances or—

Everybody does. You see somebody and say, "Oh." When I look at you, I say, "Not Harlem."

Well, I'm part Mexican and German and maybe have some black and—

Nobody sees that. You're a white guy.

Yeah. But . . . Um . . . That gives me the right to make

the comments I make! Or something like that. Because I've got the blood. Supposedly. That's what I've been told.

You mean in your culture? In Argentina?

No, no. In this country. If you say, "I believe this," people will say, "Well, you're just a white guy," so I can tell them I'm part Mexican and—

Aw, fuck *that!* That's ridiculous! Fuck it! It's *bullshit!*

It's politically correct, but it's true.

It's bullshit.

Of course it's bullshit, but—

Don't ever . . . You can make whatever commentary you want about being slaves; you can make a commentary about a bully who's going to hurt you even if you've never been beat up before and be dead-on. You don't have to experience something to know what it is.

Look, I'm just talking in terms of the current climate.

They're wrong.

Absolutely. They are.

And some people who *are* something may not have a fucking clue about what it's about, and the reverse is true too. So whattaya got?

What have I got? Okay, uh, we were yapping about the Punisher and I—

Don't put it in the equipment section. I don't *want* it in the equipment section. Put it in the article! I've gotta get—

Well, look. I'll-I'll-I'll ask. I'll ask the boss. The boss is God. The boss has to look everything over. I can make suggestions, but I'm an insignificant insect, so I can't promise you anything.

[Whistles as if he's just witnessed a car crash.] *I* would say, "He's the boss . . . for *now. I'm* the next boss. Meet the new boss."

I don't want to be the boss! I want to write novels.

But be your own boss.

Absolutely.

[Shouts triumphantly.] SEE? SEE? SAME THING!

I don't want to run a magazine, though.

Yeah, but you still want to be boss. Everybody wants to be boss.

Sure, but he's just like you. Picks up the phone, "Yes! No! Bobbitty-boppitty-bopp! 'Bye!" and slams it down. I don't want—

That's why he's the boss.

It's not worth it to me.

Look, you wanna do the same thing in your world. You wanna be the boss.

But just the boss of me. Just me and my own . . . self.

That's still a boss.

I want no acolytes; I want no entourages, no nothing. I just want to be me alone.

No plebes or plebeians, huh?

No. Wanna be left alone.

I mean, plebes or patricians.

Okay, so are you not going to tell me about your equipment because you don't like sidebars?

Oh sure! The absolute, bottom-line truth is that I've used the Punisher for the last two or three tours. For a while, they were made by B. C. Rich. There were only five made. They paid me; they went out of business, so I decided to do it myself. It just wasn't as good as what I wanted. The wood I wanted, Schaller tuning pegs, the best equipment. EMG pickups. And I wanted the old Fender bridge cover. It's sort of a hybrid of what I liked most about an instrument. I wanted the instrument to look cool and sexy and powerful instead of these mutant instruments that have one horn that's bigger than the other. I never understood that. If you look at nature and see a horned beast, very few of them have unequal parts. Every once in a while you get a lobster with one larger claw, but he looks stupid. And I think all those basses, including the Fender basses, look stupid. They have no beauty of design from just the look of it.

Why the bridge cover? Doesn't that get in the way for muting the strings?

No. I rest my case . . . I rest my hand on the bridge. And also

I've found that I don't wanna clean my instrument, so food and all kinds of stuff, sweat—it all goes into the bridge. I wanted to cover that. And I think it looks cool. Some chrome on the instrument.

What about pedals, effects?

Nothing. You can push an amp, any amp. I've used SETs [single-ended triode amplifiers], Trace Elliots, even Marshall guitar amps; they sound just as good.

And what do you use now?

Literally any combination. On some of those songs I used a Roland guitar amplifier with a twelve, so obviously I distorted it. A little handheld thing, but it sounded great. You can't use that live as well. I used a Marshall 200, a Laney, and an SET. It really doesn't matter. I defy a human being walking on the face of the planet to listen to a record and say, "Oh, that amplifier, that's a so-and-so amplifier." You can't. And it's often difficult to say, "Oh, that bass? That's a ———." Sorry. Just like when you finally get to someplace, as you're sitting here with me? I don't have a fuckin' clue what kind of car brought you here. You could have used any car. Any bass will do the job. Sorry! And any amplifier will do it.

You're dismissing millions of luthiers and—

It's taste! You know, this taste and that taste. It still does the job. That's why I think all these magazines—the guitar magazines, the tambourine magazines, drum magazines—it's complete bullshit. It's contemplating your navel. If it really is about the technical stuff, it's a waste of fuckin' time.

Why?

Because it avoids the main issue. If you fuckin' play it on a banjo or just hum it, if you've got the right sense, they will come. If you've got the tune, they will come. If you play it on a Fender, a Silvertone—and Silvertone do make a guitar, not just . . . If you play it on anything, it . . . doesn't . . . *matter!* It's really . . . *Songwriting* magazine? I get that. *Cabinetmaking* magazine? *Couch* magazine? I don't get it.

Chapter Four

So How Do You Guys Get Along?

[Side A of the tape is full. As I attend to the recorder, Gene suddenly stands and invites me into the control room, saying he wants to play me a mix of "Hate." Inside, I meet producer Toby Wright and guitarist Bruce Kulick, who are watching a Garth Brooks video on television and poring over a proofsheet of Kiss photos. A small drawing of Beavis and Butt-head in Kiss make-up has been taped to the side of one of the consoles, almost out of sight. Butt-head is wearing Simmons's Demon face, and Beavis is tricked out as Paul Stanley's Star Child.

Simmons floats around with a comfortable, proprietary air, his hands clasped in front of him. He wants to see how I do among his colleagues, apparently, so I try not to embarrass him. Kulick tells me that he loves bass guitar, and the debate about instruments picks up right where it left off. Everyone starts talking at the same time, yelling over each other and interrupting. Wright leaves at some point, having only said "Hi."]

Simmons: Creation has to come in. They're looking for paint-by-numbers. It never works. No! You've gotta go through something because that's part of the beauty of coming up with the music and the stuff and the feel. I mean, there's a great Phil Collins interview in a drum magazine. *He* was on the cover!

Drum magazine, or something. "Exclusive! The drums! The sound of the drums in 'In the Air Tonight.'" Whatever it's called. "In Your Face . . . " What's that song? Yeah, "In the Air Tonight." And it starts off, "How did you get the drums?" And he says, "Well, mate, you know, I sit behind the board with my engineer, and my engineer starts moving mics, and I say, 'Nope, I don't like it. Move it a little over there. Okay, *now* I like it.'" That's how he got the sound. That's *it! That's* the secret! "What mic did you use?" "Oh, a Soundhauser fourteen shotgun! A six-fourteen—"

Kulick: Well, maybe they should've interviewed the engineer at that session.

Simmons: *My* point is you can get *that* sound or a different sound. That song would've been great with whatever they used. It's a point of view, and they're looking for paint-by-numbers. That's the problem.

Not always. I disagree. Not always. It's not that they want to cop it or whatever.

Simmons: I say, forget it and be cool, like this kid Trent Reznor, who doesn't give a shit about what's going on. "I don't know a lot about this stuff. Let's see what happens; do it backwards; throw it against the wall. I just wanna get an emotional rise out of them."

But it doesn't hurt to tell the guys who want to know what you use. It doesn't hurt! It's no skin off your nose.

Kulick: I love reading about anyone I think is successful. Just like you [nods at Simmons] loved reading the Beatle book that explains how they did the album, what's it called, about the *Abbey Road* sessions.

Simmons: The songwriting. Not the—

Kulick: Well, you were still talking about, "Oh, they VSO'd [variable-speed oscillatored] his voice! I *knew* it!" You know, you wanna know certain things where you go, "Oh, so *that's* how they got that sound."

Simmons: Well, I'll grant you—

Kulick: It's just because you love the Beatles so much, it's interesting. I gotta admit, I don't read every word of every article, but—

Simmons: But not what setting or what instrument or what kind of pedals. It *starts* with the song! And film students—you know I went to film, ah, listened to some of the film classes at school—they got trapped in the same thing, which is, "What lens did they use?" They're missing the point. It begins with the word. And whether you use this lens or that lens, whether it's a down shot or an up shot, it's not style over substance, it's *substance!* Because if you have substance, you can use a lot of different styles to get impact.

Kulick: But you know the flavor's different when I hand you my [Gibson] EB-3, and you play that as opposed to your Punisher.

Simmons: It's a momentary mirage because when you hear the record when you buy it, you . . . don't . . . *know.* "Oh, that's a ———. 'Stairway to Heaven' [snaps fingers], got it! That's an EBO—"

Kulick: Nonmusicians don't know! But people who play instruments and copy every note, they would like to know!

I can tell when Flea **[Michael Balzary]** *uses a MusicMan StingRay and when he changes to something else and then goes back to the StingRay. The StingRay's got its own vibe. I mean, I have a StingRay, and when I bought it, I—*

Simmons: And you can tell that?

Yeah. I love it! Because it's got that StingRay vibe. I can tell you when it's a P-Bass, when it's a— And not because I'm a technohead, but because they've got their vibes.

Simmons: Well, what's wrong with technoheads? Did you just put them down?

You're putting them down!

Simmons: [In pompous voice.] "Not that I'm a technohead because I'm *above* that! I just go by the sound of things! Uh-hyuh-hyuh-hyuh-hyuh!"

No, no, no, no, no!

Kulick: [Shakes head; laughs.] Oh, man.

Simmons: [To Kulick.] I was doing his laugh. [To me.] Look, I don't think it matters. Write a song, and they will come. And then whether you record it hot or cold, you figure that because every band— Listen. [Sings from the Beatles' "Eleanor Rigby."] And then Ray Charles. [Does roaring Charles impression.] And then Aretha Franklin does it. [Honks like car horn, then takes deep breath and shouts almost full voice.] IT DOESN'T MATTER!

[Actual pin-drop silence for several seconds.]

Kulick: [Clears throat.] Ultimately it does to me because, when you're really into a band, I think every little cough, every little sneeze, every little hiccup matters.

Simmons: It's a great hobby, is what it is.

Kulick: Yeah! But if your passion is music, these are the people you grew up with.

Simmons: That's *not* the point. It's not what the music is wearing. It's the creation of the music, whether you play it on acoustic guitar, electric guitar, or whatever. The other stuff's a great hobby.

Kulick: Well, they wanna know what brushes the guy paints with!

Simmons: But it misdirects all that energy. If they spent all that time sitting there and trying to figure out what goes into songwriting or singing and not about the technical stuff or just playing, if they just learn—

Kulick: But what if the right bass sound inspires them to write songs?

Simmons: I grant you that. I think that's a good point.

Kulick: That doesn't always happen, but sometimes it does.

Simmons: I hear you. Sound can help you get into the moment. Oh yeah. [Pause.]

Um, I need to rely on you to tell me when you've had enough. Because I'll just keep going until you stop.

As long as it's a cover story, I'll blow your editor on the street to get it. I want a cover story, and if there's no cover story, I don't wanna be in *Bass* magazine.

Bass PLAYER *magazine.*

Fuck no! Otherwise what am I getting out of it? What am I getting out of it? "*Bass* magazine! Page fifty-four, Gene Simmons interview!" Fuck *off!* I don't need that shit.

Kiss, from left: Gene Simmons, Eric Singer, Paul Stanley, and Bruce Kulick

Bass PLAYER *magazine.*

Cover or nothing. [Sings from Arthur Altman and Jack Lawrence's "All or Nothing at All."] The reason I sound cocky is because I am. I don't wanna play small-time. I want big or nothing. Just like you.

Like me. Big or nothing.

Okay, turn off your little machine for a second.

[They play me a mix of "Hate" from the new studio album. It's fantastic: dark, powerful, fast, complex, very contemporary sounding. It somehow reminds me of heavier, angrier Red Hot Chili Peppers. It's the best from Kiss I've heard in years, and I decide that, if the rest of the album sounds anything like it, it'll be a huge success. I jump up and yell at Kulick, *"This is a great song!"* He smiles painfully, like he's about to cry. I take my key ring out and spin it on my finger, wondering what bloody stupid thing I've said now.

Another problem is that Gene wanders over twice to make sure that my little machine is really off. The second time, I try to pop the tape out, but he reaches down and starts pressing the FAST-FORWARD, REWIND, RECORD, and PLAY buttons in abnormal combinations. He's acting as if he's never seen a recorder in his life, staring at it with a cocked head and stabbing it so hard that it's shimmying all over the desktop, the red light flashing.

"What's up?" I shout, too afraid to slap his hand away. "What're you doing?"

He glances at me and slowly closes his eyes, lifting his left shoulder in an elaborate shrug; he stops tampering with my recorder, though. Later, I discover that he's erased or garbled part of our debate about technical matters. The tape doesn't pick up any music, just loud smacking sounds like very enthusiastic . . . kisses.

When the song is over, the discussion of equipment continues. I mention to Simmons that I can tell he didn't use his Punisher on "Hate" because the instrument sounds much brighter, much more trebly. He says nothing for a few seconds and then admits that he used a Pedulla bass. This makes me feel guilty. I almost apologize but decide we should just go back to the interview.]

So you're in here finishing up your next studio album.
Simmons: Toby Wright: producer. Bruce Kulick: songwriter, guitar player. [To Kulick.] See? You're a songwriter.
Kulick: Thank you.
Simmons: Singer too.
Kulick: [Laughs.] Right! I sing one song.
So did this album work out from jams and riffs?
Simmons: Pieces. Bridges. Choruses. Oh, there must have been at least five different versions of this song.
So you have three songwriters now. Is that a problem in terms of one person stamping all over everyone else?

Simmons: Naah. Everybody's got a big mouth. If they don't like something, they speak up. I said this before, but Bruce really made a quantum leap forward. Everybody's got the ability to do, I think, their best, but you've gotta have the balls to step up to your point of view. Until two years ago, Bruce has been a nice guy, and now he's turned into a complete prick. If he doesn't like something, he goes up and says, "That's horrible! What were you thinking?" You know what? The truth is, you will get the respect you demand. He steps up to the plate, and you see passion and emotion behind the opinion, no matter how coarse or disagreeable you think an opinion is. Who cares who's right?

Kulick: One thing about this band is that everyone gets a chance to have their say. Everyone's ideas will be tried. We want to try them all because we're never sure. But then obviously the best thing *does* wind up on the— We'll take the janitor's suggestion.

Simmons: Well, you wanna save the new album for another article, don't you? Now: Call the article, "Cover or Nothing."

Okay. **[Into tape recorder.]** *Gene Simmons suggests we call the article "Cover or Nothing." Now, I have a question that I'm sure won't offend you, after spending the last couple hours with you.*

How long is my dick?

No. Do you think your method of operation instills in the end maybe a little contempt for your fellow humans?

On my side or towards me?

On your side.

No. No. Absolutely not. I really have very strong philosophical, ethical points of view about everything. I just think hate is natural, and love has to be worked at. So since the tendency of man is to be lazy, usually what you look at if you say something off-color in a bar someplace is a sock in the face, not "I beg your pardon; I'd like to discuss this thing because I know you didn't really mean it." Nobody is going to give you the benefit of the doubt, by and large. And I go back to what I said before: You and I are completely the same because you and I look both ways when we cross the street. Not because we expect to be hit by a car but because chances are some guy is gonna hit you.

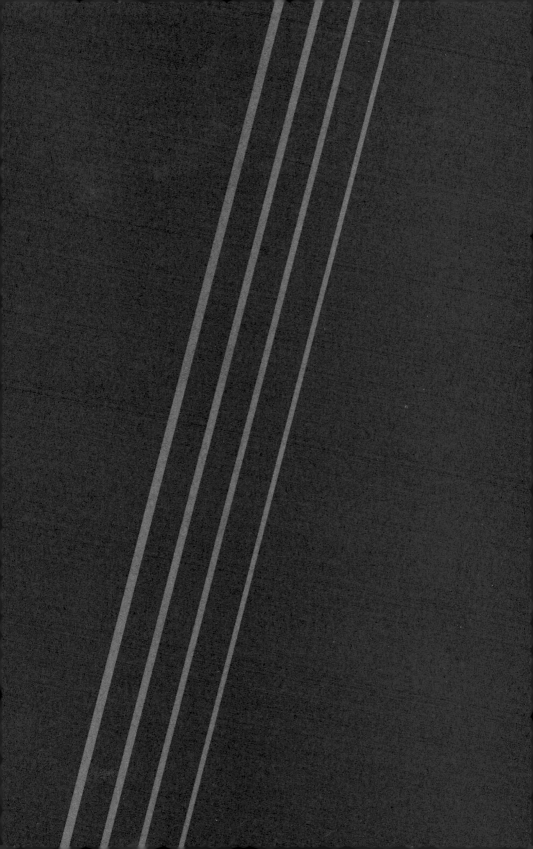

Chapter Five
Encore! Encore!

All righty. If it's going to be a cover story, they're probably going to want stuff to transcribe. Do you have any favorite bass lines you'd want transcribed?

What kind of favorites?

Lines that you'd want transcribed.

Into Russian? What?

No! To put down on a piece of staff paper that shows all the notes. Half steps, whole steps, quarter notes, and all that.

Kulick: Show 'em your bass line for "Detroit Rock City" [*Destroyer*].

Exactly. If you have . . . If you can give me three, maybe they'll choose one from them. They'll either do sections or—

Simmons: Oh. *They'll* do this.

Well, yeah. You don't have to do it.

Because I can't . . . You know, 90 percent . . . I'm guessing the vast majority of people can't read or write music.

Kulick: They get like a Steve Vai type to transcribe all the notes.

Right. Then they put a tablature underneath it. So it's probably a waste of time asking you, but if you can indulge us—

Simmons: No, I think . . . I actually think that that stuff is really important because, if you can read it, you get a chance to study song structure. *That's* the study part.

So if you can't think of anything right now—

You mean for bass?

Yes! Bass lines! What they'll do is have a guy named Karl Coryat, who'll annotate it, saying things like, "His tasty use of ghost notes here is what propels the song forward," or something like that.

Kulick: Right away, something like "Detroit Rock City" comes to mind. You have a riff that no one else plays. I'm trying to think of some others.

You can think about it and tell me later.

Simmons: Nah, it doesn't matter. Let's pick some now. Even though "Unholy" *[Revenge]* shadows the guitar, it's really not . . . The bass lines that I like are the ones that are not trapped by the kick, like that pumping . . . I like the ones that are doing their own thing. Especially "Going Blind."

Kulick: Yeah, that's perfect.

Do you like "Tough Love" **[Revenge]?**

Simmons: No.

Kulick: That one follows the guitar.

Simmons: There's a song called "Going Blind," that's going to be on the *Unplugged* record, that was actually off of . . . You can grab it off of the second album *[Hotter Than Hell]*. That bass line has nothing to do with the chordal structure or the rhythmic structure. It's almost reminiscent of the line in "Michelle," where it's a melody. It's different than the verse melody, different than the guitars, and different than the rhythm structure underneath.

Okay. Are we at two? Did you say "Going Blind" and "Unholy"?

Kulick: Ah, I just threw that one out there. "Strutter" *[Kiss]* you run around a lot on too, don't you? [Sings bass line from "Strutter."] It's got that kind of rock and roll feel. "Rock and Roll All Nite" *[Dressed to Kill]* has got another good bass line. It's a very clever bass line.

Simmons: Similar to "Strutter."

Kulick: Yeah, well, you don't have to say "Strutter." I still think, for me, for the classic stuff, "Detroit" was always a great riff. I mean, I don't care if it's all classic stuff. I'm not sure if in any of the other stuff the bass is that separate from the verse.

Simmons: Okay, so "Detroit" could be a good bass line, and I think "Unholy." So you have "Going Blind," "Detroit," and "Unholy."

All right. What they might also do is choose sections from each of three songs, like they did the last guy who got the cover. What's his name? I can't think of his name.

[Van Halen's] Michael Anthony?

No, after that. He used to play with Japan [Mick Karn].

Oh, Ira Lippschitz.

No, from the band Japan! You remember Japan, from the eighties? Have you ever heard of them?

Well, I know who that is. David Sylvian. But they're completely unknown in this country.

Right. But he's a great bass player.

But that's another subject. We were just talking about . . . You said, "Have you ever heard of them?" We were on whether or not he's famous. And when we said, "He's not famous," you said, "Yes, but he's great." You know what I mean, that's like another—

I prefer quality to fame.

I'll take fame first. If you're—

If you've got the quality—

[Raises index finger.] You didn't let me finish what I was going to say. If you're brilliant and completely unknown, it's the saddest thing in the world. The best of all possible worlds is to be talented and enormously famous. It's not a negative. People actually recognize that you're famous. It is possible to be famous and not great. But the best of all possible worlds is to be famous and talented. Or talented and famous. The saddest thing is to be talented, and nobody gives a shit.

[Examines me for a few seconds.] Actually, you find that appealing somehow, I think.

Well, yeah. I do.

You don't want people to recognize your greatness.

No, I don't. I'm crazy, I know. [Laughing.] I'm afraid of fans. I'm afraid of fame and power.

OVERLEAF— *Gene Simmons (left), Paul Stanley, and Peter Criss*

And you know, I thank God for guys like you because it gives me the chance to grab bigger and bigger audiences, and I *love* that.

That's fine. Go for it. I just want enough to pay the rent.

No. *No!* Don't go halfway. You know, it's qualifying between famous and unknown. But I guess you're right. You can be unknown and still pay the rent.

Well, I guess that's about it. I'd like to say—

That you're thankful. You were enlightened. You had a great time.

I turned the recorder off. Simmons shook my hand and expelled me from the control room, telling me I'd better make the article a cover story because he needed to buy his mother a new house. I went back to the lounge for my jacket and bag and found Toby Wright sprawled on the sofa staring at the ceiling, a cigarette clamped between his teeth. "Keeee-*rist!*" I yelled at him. "Tell me about it," he intoned, not looking at me. When I walked out of the lounge, I saw a tall, gorgeous Eurasian woman in her early twenties being escorted into the control room. She was wearing leather trousers, spike heels, a tight black coat with wide shoulder pads, and a dreamy expression. I passed by the open studio door and glimpsed Simmons embracing her stiffly, like a peace envoy. She snuggled into his chest, her arms dangling by her sides; he was facing her but watching me from the corners of his eyes, a subtle Mona Lisa smile curving his lips.

A few days later, after I'd transcribed the interview, I sent a list of follow-up questions to Mercury. Gene phoned from his office and refused to answer any of them. They were mostly about his background, how many languages he spoke and so on. "Why would you need to know that?" he demanded. "Put down I know just enough to get laid in fifteen different countries." He also refused to tell me anything more about his equipment.

He was rustling papers around and said he had me on the

speaker so he could catch up on his work. "This way too," he added, "I don't have to . . . *hold* you . . . as I talk to you," giving the word "hold" a campy, insinuating emphasis. I thanked him for putting another lovely image in my head, but he was already moving on to his thirty-record discography, which he dictated at warp speed. I struggled along with my pen, my hand cramping as I wrote nonsense like *Httr n Hll, Crechrs o Nite, Aliv 1*. I knew I could look the titles up later, so I don't understand why I bothered, unless it was because he'd told me to do it and I'd gotten used to obeying him. I wouldn't have had to write anything if my tape recorder had been hooked up to the telephone, of course, but once again his call had been completely unexpected.

After we finished with the discography, we had the following exchange, which is reconstructed from memory:

You really hate talking on the phone, don't you?

No. Now, Tom, I kid everyone, including myself. I pull people's legs all the time, but I'm not kidding now. This is very important to me. I need to know: Did I get the cover or not?

Honest to God, no kidding, you got the cover. My boss says, if the interview is as good as I say it is, you're going right on the cover. He promised.

Well, I can tell you this because there's no one else around; I'm all by myself in my office, and no one can hear me. This is my job. It's my job to piss people off. I have to do it because it's what's expected of me. It's what people want. And I'd like to say I think you're a great guy and a lot of fun to be with, and I had a lot of fun talking to you. I really enjoyed myself. I hope you go on to write lots of best-selling novels and make lots and lots of money. More than *enough* money. Make tons of the stuff and find happiness and success.

Well, thank you very much.

Go out and write; get everything you want; do everything you want to do; have a great writing career. Goodbye.

Coda

After the article had been submitted, but before it was published, I learned that Kiss might be planning a reunion tour with the two long-departed original members, drummer Peter Criss and guitarist Ace Frehley. Simmons had mentioned nothing of the sort, and if it were true, my piece would be a disaster. As much as I hate to admit this, I'd gone more or less bonkers praising what I'd heard of the studio album: "A new direction for Kiss. Still growing after twenty-five years. You'd never know it was the same band." And so on. It would be an unmitigated fiasco.

I sent queries to Gene's fax and P.O. box numbers, praying that it was all just zany Internet gossip. When I got no answer, I contacted Mercury Records and was told by a publicist that they could neither confirm nor deny any such rumors. I rode out the sickening rush of déjà vu and asked if Mercury wanted me to be accurate or not. Since a reunion would be huge news, I'd have to completely redo the article, maybe even reinterview Simmons. At the very least, I needed up-to-date information. "I under*stand* that," the young fellow in New York said. "We can neither confirm nor deny any such rumors."

A few weeks later, I determined that the reunion was indeed going to happen, so I called Jim Roberts and asked him what to do. He'd already pulled the piece off the presses for a last-minute rewrite, he told me, but he was going to go ahead and let it run in the July '96 issue. Soon after it came out, Bruce Kulick and drummer Eric Singer quit Kiss. They had no real jobs anyway, now that Kiss Mark One was back. The studio album, eventually titled *Carnival of Souls,* was in limbo, everybody on the planet waiting to see if the original lineup would make their first record in almost twenty years. Not surprisingly, they did, releasing *Psycho Circus* in 1998. As for *Carnival,* either Kulick or Singer was alleged to have said, "Oh, it's in the can, all right—the garbage can." It finally appeared in 1997, barely publicized and graced with what might be the glummest band photos ever taken.

Though my interview contributed to the deluge of hype engulfing Kiss in the late spring and early summer of 1996, it was the only cover story that virtually ignored the reunion tour. I *wish* I could say that I'd had incredible foresight, a master plan for making my piece stand out, but the truth is, I didn't know about any reunion because nobody had bothered to tell me.

Part Two
Peter Hook
August 12, 1997

Chapter Six
Relax, Mate

The interview was scheduled for 3:00 P.M. at the El Rey Theatre on Wilshire Boulevard in Los Angeles, but Peter Hook was three hours late. While waiting around, I drank too much coffee and tried to decide whether or not I should abort. Even though I wasn't a huge fan of techno-pop or synth-dance or Euro-disco or whatever, I was intrigued by New Order, Hook's former band. They rarely gave interviews and were supposed to be drug-soaked fascists who'd driven themselves mad through their excesses and isolation. Formed from the ashes of Joy Division after the suicide of lead singer Ian Curtis in 1980, New Order had been at the forefront of British club culture. They set the standards for an entire genre of music, popularizing the twelve-inch single and making extensive use of the new computer and sequencer technology while retaining a human, even raw, sound. Critics generally regarded them as one of the most important links between seventies dance and eighties house music.

Significance and controversy aside, the main reason I was drawn to New Order was their misspent potential. Loved by reviewers and blessed with rabidly devoted fans, they still never topped the success of their breakthrough smash hit "Blue Monday," the best-selling twelve-inch of all time. They were media stars in Britain but hadn't caught on in the United States except as a cult band, possibly because under the snappy electronic drums and burbling synthesizers the lyrics were uniformly morose. The stark packaging of the records perpetuated a cold, distant image, and when a notoriously erratic live show and a refusal to do encores were thrown in, the result was an act that just didn't endear itself to the average American listener. There was also persistent innuendo of totalitarian leanings, an allegation stemming in part from the band names themselves: "Joy Divisions" were the forced brothels in Nazi death camps, and "the New Order" was what Cambodian genocideur Pol Pot called his rule.

Low Life was mentioned repeatedly in my references as a model for the British dance scene of the late eighties and early nineties, but every time New Order seemed to be getting back on track, a rumor would surface that they were breaking up. Someone was always unhappy no matter which direction they were going, and they rarely capitalized on the momentum they'd built. When this interview took place in 1997, it wasn't clear if the quartet was still active, the British music press reporting that the relentless "internal tensions" had finally done it in. True or not, the members were all off on solo projects, and their former label, Factory Records, had collapsed four years earlier.

In keeping with New Order's reputation as innovators, Peter Hook was a unique bass guitarist. He was one of the few who could accurately be called a "lead bassist," which isn't to say that he fired off a million notes per second à la guitarist Eddie Van Halen. What he did instead was play simple, effective, twangy melodies in the upper registers, the actual bass lines usually provided by a keyboard or sequencer. Every interviewer asked him about it, and his answer was always the same, that he started doing it because higher notes were easier for him to hear, especially when all the other instruments were going. I resolved not to bring it up. I did want to ask how the electric bass–synth bass combination worked in a live context, and I wanted to know how he'd made the change in style from his Joy Division days, when he was a relatively orthodox bassist. I also wanted to touch on his own band, Revenge, a defunct "hard rock–dance outfit" that had been murdered by the critics and completely ignored by the public.

In retrospect, it was probably the caffeine that prompted me to stick it out. I was overheated and *very* optimistic, convinced he'd gladly make up for my wasted time after he saw how patient I'd been. With nothing else to do, I reread the press kit supplied by Polydor Records. All the clippings were from British magazines or newspapers, and they concentrated on Hook's titanic drinking, his brawling, his failed marriage to British television comedienne Caroline Aherne, and a recent public encounter he'd had with her new boyfriend. This particular scuffle had been caught on film, the writers dissecting it blow by blow in the most mind-bogglingly cynical prose I'd ever come across: "The punch that rocked Manchester!" "Hello, old fist!" "A left, a right, another right! Oh, *dear!*"

With sledgehammer irony, they used all sorts of cute nicknames too, including the grotesque diminutive "Hooky," "The Beast," and "The Lizard King," a recycled moniker that was supposed to invoke the sleaze and miasma of Jim Morrison, I guess. I'd always loved Britain, but these articles were absolutely foul in their giggling snideness. They were also incomprehensible. One interview was peppered with the word(?) "Heeurgh!" and the rest contained huge wads of Mancunian dialect. I later looked the word "Mancunian" up and discovered that it was an adjective used to describe someone or something from Manchester, Hook's hometown.

Hook finally strolled in at six o'clock, his hair bleached a startling blond-white. A young woman staggered along behind him, clutching a case of Heineken to her chest. I stood up, and the tour manager, a tall, heavyset, damp-looking Brit, approached and said, "Right: You've got twenty minutes." Stunned, I explained that I wanted to write a feature-length article, an in-depth study of this iconoclastic, two-fisted ex-dockworker with the strange style of playing. The tour manager just said, "Sorry. That's all the time we can spare." I asked if there was any way we could reschedule. He shook his head. "Can't be done. This is it." Then he walked away.

Peter Hook ambled over and pressed my hand, sipping from

a bottle of beer. I told him that we couldn't possibly do a good interview in twenty minutes; he shrugged and said nothing. With no other alternative except just turning around and walking out, I began a frantic search for a quiet place. Hook followed at a stately pace, drinking his Heineken, one hand in the pocket of his shorts. I was marvelously aware that all my notes on New Order, Joy Division, and Revenge were useless. We'd have to concentrate on Monaco, the duo he'd formed with guitarist David "Pottsy" Potts, but since I didn't really like their album, *Music for Pleasure,* I had no idea what to ask. I'd been assigned to do a profile, not an ad for a new product, my editor having told me to "get this guy's story."

The full sound check suddenly started, making the theater as noisy as a boiler factory. We tried standing in the earsplitting lobby and then moved out onto the sidewalk in front of the building. I turned my tape recorder on because we'd already used up one precious minute.

Since we only have twenty minutes, we have to get started. **[Thundering passage of truck.]** *Jesus. What about those VIP rooms, or the bathroom, or anything? I mean, since we only have twenty minutes!*

[We go back into lobby and find theater manager.]
Hook: [To theater manager.] We're doing an interview, and we need someplace to go.
A place to talk!
Theater Manager: A quiet place to do an interview . . . Come up to the kitchen.
Cool.
[Tape picks up several seconds of footsteps as we make our way up long flight of wooden stairs to second floor.]
Theater Manager: How many guys are coming up?
Just two.
Theater Manager: I can probably get you a couple chairs.
Come on over here. It's not aesthetically pleasing, but who'll

ever know? [Brings in two chairs, putting them next to metal-topped counter.]

It's perfect.

Hook: Thank you very much.

[Theater manager leaves. Hook and I sit down. I glance through my notes.]

Twenty minutes. We've got twenty minutes to go over twenty years.

Twenty *years?* Nobody told me we were going over twenty years. [Laughs.]

Well, but—

That'd take a hell of a long time, wouldn't it?

Well, it's supposed to be a feature article, and looking over all this material here, it's just, kind of a . . . Well, okay. It seems like, especially the British press, seems to mostly talk about you as a person and almost never mentions your music.

I think that's pretty much the British press. [Laughs.] With every band, I think. They're more interested in my marriage than my music.

Well, it's a shame because in those twenty years, you've pretty much done everything as a bassist. So . . . I guess, uh . . . [Shuffling notes desperately.] Um, uh . . .

[Pats me on shoulder.] Relax. Relax. Relax.

Okay. Tell me about, uh . . . Goddamn. I'm just kind of flustered.

Well, don't— Don't be flustered. Relax. You must've known what you're going to ask.

Sure. Okay. I guess the most important thing from a bassist's point of view is, you seem to go from genre to genre, and—

[Sharply.] In which way? In which way?

In which way? Okay, the Monaco album. What is it, the single? You have the single, but if you compare that to, oh, I don't know, um, like "Sweet Lips," or, or—

"Buzz Gum."

Yeah, okay. That.

Things like that. Yeah. You mean the versatility of it. The difference in style.

Yeah. Yeah.

Um . . . Oh, God. I don't know. I mean, thinking about New Order, I think it was pretty much the same anywhere. There was a lot of different styles. There's some very melodic and some quite rhythmic. It was always quite driven, I suppose. And— I don't know. The thing is, I very rarely think about what I do, anyway. I just do it. I don't think, "Well, this will be a rocky one; this one's gonna be this; that one's gonna be that." You just sort of evolve, and you do them differently. My main interest, I suppose, is being melodic. More than anything else, it's the melodies that I find interesting. I don't find rhythm work— I mean, I know I'm not a bass player in what is generally termed "bass playing." Just generally root notes? I can't do that.

Well, some of the stuff you do, like "Sweet Lips," has . . . Well, it's hard to tell if, it's—

That's a keyboard.

Oh. Okay, are you playing that, or is somebody else?

No, I play that. [Sings.] *Duh-dit, dih-dit-dih, doo-duh, dih-dih-rit, duh-rit, dih-dih-dit, doo-rit, dih-dwih-rit.*

But there's a bass guitar in there too, isn't there?

Yeah, that *boom-ditn-dwoo-rit, doom-bitn.* That's just a disco rip-off that Pottsy did. Pottsy played that.

So you switch back and forth between keyboards and electric bass?

Yeah. I mean I, I write keyboard. I can't play it, but I do write it. I'm probably one of the world's worst musicians. I can't tune up. I'm tone-deaf. I can write songs, but I can't play them. Once I've written a riff, I can't find it on the keyboard or fretboard.

So what do you do then?

Pottsy shows me where it is. Then, when I get it in me head, I can do it.

So I guess you're self-taught, then.

Yeah. When I first began, I went to see the Sex Pistols. See, I'd never had anything to do with a musical instrument ever in my life. Until I was twenty-one, I had no interest in it whatsoever. I was interested in music for the buzz of it. [Belches.] And for the groups. But I wasn't into it for a musical thing. I didn't know anything about playing an instrument, and I didn't even want to, really. It never crossed me mind to buy an instrument. Never. I was just plodding me way through life, as you do, wondering what you're gonna do next and where you're gonna go and shit and, you know, just going out and working all week just to pay for Friday night and Saturday night. And I went to see the Sex Pistols, and there was something about what they did. It wasn't particularly musical because it sounded *awful.* It was really bad. So it wasn't anything to do with music. It was just some . . . It was like seein' the job that you wanted to do after all those years of seeing your careers officer at school and working your way through jobs and everything and all that shit, and you actu-

ally found what you wanted to do. I thought, "Fuck it. That's what I want to do!" But it wasn't for a musical reason. And the next day I went out and bought a bass guitar because Bernard [Sumner, the future guitarist of Joy Division and New Order] had a lead guitar, electric guitar.

And then when I bought it, I thought, "What the *fuck* am I gonna do with this thing?" I went and bought a book, 'cause Bernard had the same book, which was the Palmer–Hughes book of rock and roll bass guitar, where you stuck the notes on your neck. That was really good because then you knew where the notes were. And that was it. I started learning, and then I got bored with learning because it was taking too long, and I just started playing with Bernard. We started writing our first punk things and evolved from there.

Lots of people have talked about Joy Division being much darker than Monaco. There's a quote from you here, where you said music is pure emotion for you.

Mm-hmm. [Long pause.]

Okay. Do you find your emotions going from dark to light and back again when you're writing? Or does it—

Uh, no. I don't know about that. I mean, I find some music quite moving. I find "Shine," particularly, on this album, uplifting. I find "Sedona" very melancholy, so it does bring out an emotion in me, you know. It depends, doesn't it? I mean, one day you come in, and you're a bit pissed off and a bit upset about something, and you write a melancholy song. But if you're feeling like this [moves shoulders and hips as if dancing], you write an up-tempo song. I suppose your emotions *do* sort of dictate what you do.

Right. A lot of people seemed to be surprised at this album. I mean, at least according to these mostly British press clips, you're sort of the bad boy of pop music—

[Laughs loudly.]

—and you surprised everyone by coming out with this—

Good record?

Well, this happy record.

OPPOSITE— *Peter Hook (left), and Ian Curtis of Joy Division*

[Laughs; shakes head.]

I mean, I think everyone agrees that your music was always good, but now it's "happy and light!" That sort of thing.

Aaaah, I think the lyrics are quite dark. But that's a different aspect of it that doesn't have anything to do with the bass. I don't know; I guess you get to a stage in your life where, I don't know, you feel good, and this is my stage for that. I mean, I was going through several different kinds of hell writing the record, but I think the thing was, it kept me optimistic doing it. [Belches.] I saw a vision because I had this germ of an idea that Pottsy and I could make a good record. I'd heard the record we could make. I think that kept me going. That emotion kept you going. So regardless of all the low periods you had, it kept you up there and gave you a focus for your life. An optimistic focus. I didn't want it to be completely miserable or anything. I made sure it was okay. So, um, I suppose from *that* aspect it did. But, uh, I mean, it's just the strength that gave me strength in myself, and you know, the strength in myself went through for that.

Chapter Seven
Those Things You Do

So . . . Okay, since I'm writing for a bass magazine, let's talk about that. A lot has been written about your technique, playing up in the high frets and all that. Um, that story seems to be pretty well known. But just listening to Monaco and a lot of the other stuff, it seems that you're doing a lot more on the bass than you sort of want to admit.

You mean, I'm playing modest? [Laughs.]

Well, you're not precisely the thug—musically—you make yourself out to be and people make you out to be. It seems like there's a lot more going on there.

Musically? [Laughs.] Well, yeah, the thing is, on the New Order stuff, you weren't just a bass player, you were a producer as well. I've never just been a bass player; I don't just play the bass. I suggest keyboard parts; I suggest orders and things like that; so musically, there is a lot going on. That technique you bring to Monaco. Musically, you'll find something that enhances the bass, or you'll change something that makes the bass better. I mean, the bass is my primary love, if you like. I like singing because I find that as an expression, people pick up on it straight away. You know, it's like that. You can get to people straight away. Playing bass guitar, you can't get an emotion out. You can make 'em rock or make 'em dance; you can make 'em melancholy or make them uplifted or whatever, but it's not like talking words to somebody. And I didn't discover that until Revenge. But I do actually like that; I like that aspect of music now, the fact that singing can get to somebody straight away.

Did you do much singing before?

Never. Sang two songs for New Order very early on, but never any since. We used to work on the lyrics and vocal lines together. It's that thing about—where you do a lot of things and not just . . . [Pause.]

Okay. Right now, you're writing songs with your partner, and you're credited with—

[Frowns and points to open kitchen door, through which sound check is blasting.] Could you shut that door?

Oh. Yeah.

[I get up and shut the door. Two seconds later, the theater manager comes in, leaving the door wide open again. Hook immediately leaps up and slams it with emphasis. The theater manager grins at him.]

Theater Manager: [Shouts.] It's getting quite loud out there, isn't it?

Yup. It's even louder in here, it seems like, with all the metal surfaces.

[Theater manager leaves, closing door behind him.]

So, you said . . .

Go ahead.

Yeah. You said you're a producer and singer-songwriter now. Do you draw on different skills to do all that, or does it all come from the same place?

Well, I think if you're interested in it all, it comes anyway. If you're a little bit ambitious, you're going to do that anyway. Also, if you want it right. When we started Joy Division, Bernard and I in particular had a very strong idea of what we wanted it to sound like. But when [Factory Records president] Tony Wilson brought [producer] Martin Hannett in, Martin Hannett had a completely different idea of what he wanted us to sound like. Me and Bernard fought for what we wanted right from the word go. Martin Hannett would be in the middle of the desk, and I would be on that side, and Bernard would be on that side, and I'd be going [whispers], "It's your turn. You ask him." "No, you ask him. Go ahead. Tell him the hi-hat's a bit quiet," and I'd go, "Ah, the hi-hat's a bit quiet, Martin," and he'd go [roars through clenched teeth], "Why don't you fucking SHUT UP you musician swack!" We'd sit there a bit, and I'd go, "Martin, the guitar seems a bit low," and he'd go, "Fucking shut your TRAP, you manky bastard!" It used to be like that all the time, until the end, as he went through and Martin got really badly into drugs, which never do you any good whatsoever when you're working in the studio, in my opinion. We just decided we could do it ourselves. Bernard and I decided we could do it better. Also, we wanted to get rid of him because he was making us very unhappy. His way of working was making us unhappy. We weren't happy with it. We just thought it was too fey, too wimpy, the sound. The thing is, if you look at *Unknown Pleasures,* which is like one of the most revered albums in the history of music, I don't like it. I don't like the sound of it.

Why not?

Because it's too . . . It's not how I envisioned Joy Division. Or how Bernard envisioned it. But that's a taste thing, you see. [Belches.] If we had made the record sound the way Bernard and I wanted it to, it might not have sold a carrot. You know? So there is a magic involved. But the thing is, we just couldn't work with Martin anymore because we felt . . . To my mind, as a producer, when a group writes a record, and you come in as a producer, you get paid for it and give them the benefit of your experience, but you don't lay the law down. When I [produced] the Stone Roses, and I did "Elephant Stone" *[The Stone Roses],* we disagreed on a point, but the thing is, I would never do to a group what Martin Hannett did to me, which was make me unhappy with a record I have to live with the rest of my life. I have to live with *Unknown Pleasures,* and I don't like it! I wouldn't do that to the Stone Roses, and if we disagreed on a point, I'd say, "Right. Okay. It's *your* record, primarily. If that's what you want. In my opinion, this is what you should do, but if you don't want to do it, I'll go with you." To my mind, you see, it's *their* record, not *your* record. You're there to guide them.

What happened with Martin Hannett was that Martin Hannett taught me and Bernard how to do it, and as soon as me and Bernard had learned how to do it, we got rid of him. [Laughs.] And then we made all our mistakes, like on "Temptation" *[Substance]*, having the snare drum come to the left because we just didn't know. Shit like that. We made loads and loads of mistakes, but we learned how to do it. We went and did it. It became very important to me when we were working to see it through from beginning to end.

Like when we started recording, I was always the one who was always there, right the way through—through all the mixing—and the other three would come in and just make suggestions. It was always me and the engineer that worked because I felt that it was very important to be there all the time. What happened was that the group decided they didn't like that way of

working. They wanted an impartial manager. Because basically the group went off the bass. They went off the bass. They felt that two melodies were confusing. They didn't want as much bass as I wanted, so they had to bring somebody impartial to do it because basically we just argued all the time. So Stephen Hague came in, and basically he took that away from me. To my mind, that's why *Republic* doesn't particularly sound like New Order. Sounds a bit like New Order but not true New Order as in the way that *Technique* did to me. *Technique* was our finest moment.

So . . . A lot of people think Music for Pleasure *sounds more like true New Order than some of your more recent work.*

Yeah, I think that's fair. The thing was, in Revenge, I actually made a conscious effort to not sound like New Order. It had taken away me livelihood and stopped me touring and playing all the lovely songs I used to love and stopped me seeing all these lovely countries I used to see. I made a decision I didn't want to sound like them, and I tried my best to not sound like them. Which was good in a way because it taught me to look at things in a different way. Also, I had to learn to sing and write songs, which I'd never particularly done before on my own. Never. So it taught me to do things in a different way, but it didn't feel right. It wasn't like 100 percent right. It took Pottsy, when he came back, to say to me, "Why are you doin' it this way? That's not how you normally do it. You should do songs the way you used to do them in New Order. You used to base them around the bass," and shit like that. And so he got me back into doing it, and I found the pride of what I'd done.

Yeah, there's a quote that you said you had to get away from New Order and the bass elements because you weren't confident.

It wasn't that I wasn't confident; it was just that I wanted to strike out. It was like cuttin' me mother's apron strings. It's like some people leave home, don't they, but take the washing home every week so that mum can do it. Shit like that. It was my way of not taking me washing home.

OPPOSITE— *Monaco from left: Peter Hook and David Potts*

So you did stop playing bass?

Yeah. No. I mean, I played bass, but I played it in a different way. I didn't go for it in the way I did it in New Order. I just tried to do something different, but it wasn't natural, and it didn't work. It was okay, though, and I still think Revenge were an okay band. I still think we had some really good songs. But it wasn't . . . It didn't make me feel 100 percent happy. Monaco does make me 100 percent happy.

Just because you're in control, or . . .

No, because I'm doing what comes naturally again, in the way that I used to do in New Order. I'm not forcing anything; I'm not doing something that I shouldn't be doing. This is a very natural way of writing. "Shine" is a very natural Peter Hook–written song. So is "What Do You Want from Me?"

What's your writing process like?

Mostly jams. Bernard will— Bernard? *That's* a Freudian slip there, isn't it? I mean, *David* [Potts] will go in and work something out on the computer, you know, get a computer thing going, and then we'll come in and mostly wipe it away with the acoustic instruments. That's what makes us happiest . . . the acoustic and electric instruments, the electric guitar and the bass. So we'll dump all the keyboards and just make it rockier. Which is what happened on the album.

You still ended up with some of the original keyboard tracks?

Yeah, a couple. It's nice for variety. I like junk.

Well, it's really bizarre because when you hear a tune like "Sweet Lips,"—

You think it's a separate band.

—you picture a bunch of thin French kids with the sides of their heads shaved, hunched over sequencers.

[Laughs loudly.] Well, the thing is, Pottsy was very "instrumental"—excuse the pun—in doing that because he'd worked in a record shop. I don't even listen to music myself. I'm not a great fan of music, really. I only listen to dance music on the radio. I don't . . . I'm not one of these . . . I'm not really precious about it. I'm very lackadaisical. But David had worked in a record shop,

and he'd hear loads of records all day, and he was always bringing stuff back and saying, "Oh, we should try and do stuff like
this." There ended up being all these varied influences on all these
songs, which I liked. In the old days, the way that New Order used
to do it, you'd have a song that didn't have a chorus, or you'd have
a song that was an instrumental or a song that was ten minutes
long. Things like that. We'd take a lot more chances earlier on
than I thought we did when it got towards the end of New Order.

I saw a documentary about the history of rock and roll
in which you were interviewed at length, and New Order
was highlighted as one of these incredibly influential
bands. I mean, do you feel that way?

Um, I mean, I can see that. I don't know how you're supposed
to feel when you do something like that. [Laughs.] As I was just
explaining to David today, I mean, just because you're, you know,
an "innovative bass player who's influenced hundreds and hundreds of bass players," when you've got a flat tire on your car, or
when you're trying to stop your baby crying, or when you're trying to feed your dog or something, it isn't particularly any use
whatsoever, is it? In the majority of your life, it doesn't do you
much. It's a nice little thing—"Oh, great, he's influenced a thousand bass players. Great." Doesn't change your life.

Pride?

Hmm?

Pride?

Well, I don't . . . It doesn't make me proud; it makes me
embarrassed, mostly. I don't like people to say things like that to
me. I don't know how to handle it. It's not in me to say [shouts],
"Yeah, man, I'm fucking great, and I'm fucking proud of it!" I'm not
like that. [Laughs.]

Okay, quiet pride.

No. No. Not really. I don't know. I don't know. I get really
embarrassed by it. The only time it's ever— It's never bothered
me, anybody imitating my style, like [the bassists] in Everything But the Girl or Cocteau Twins or the Cure did. Loads of
people— Loads of people have done it. It's never actually
bothered me. The only time it ever actually physically bothered

me was when I went to see the Cure, and I saw that the cunt was actually fucking doing it like that [mimes his famous bass-down-by-the-ankles style]. It really bothered me because that was *real* imitation. Too *much* imitation. I don't mind them sounding like me because that's quite flattering. I think "flattery" is a much different word than "pride." I'm flattered by that. It's not something I dwell on. I wouldn't wear a T-shirt that said that. [Laughs.] You know? And I'm proud of the fact that I've worked hard and achieved something, but you have to be careful, I suppose. But that was the only time I've ever been irked by it, was when I saw [Simon Gallup] play live. Everybody always says, "You know, that guy in the Cure just ripped you off." I mean, the guy in Inspiral Carpets used to do it. Have you seen any Inspiral Carpets?

[Lying.] *Yeah.*

I actually got a tenner off him for doing it. I said, "Give me a tenner, you cunt, you've been ripping me"—as a joke—"you've been ripping me off." And I got a tenner off him! [Laughs.] Took it off him. And everyone was going, "You *gotta* be pissed, you bastard." And his girlfriend comes and says [whines drunkenly], "We can't get 'ome! We've got no money for a taxi! Can we 'ave that tenner back?" [Laughs.]

Did you give it back?

Yeah, of course. So you know, I mean, it's . . . I-I-I am flattered by it, of course. I am flattered by what New Order achieved; but in all honesty, if it wasn't for Bernard, I don't think my sound would have evolved as it did. Because it was Bernard that persuaded me to get the chorus pedal; it was Bernard that persuaded me to buy the six-string bass. Bernard has a vision that sometimes I lack. I mean, it was me who did it, though. I played and developed the style and stuff, but it was nice to get guidance.

Well, you said you can't tune a bass, you're tone-deaf, and now—

That may be a little bit of laziness. In fact, that may be a *lot* of laziness. [Laughs.] It doesn't come to me easily, you see. I can't tune . . . I *know* when it's out of tune. I can hear that, but I just can't—

New Order from left—Bernard Sumner, Gillian Gilbert, Stephen Morris, and Peter Hook

So how much of your sound, then, is actually you? I mean, do other people tell you what to play? How much comes from you?

Nobody, *nobody* tells me what to play! I hate it. I hate it when people go [whines nasally], "Why don't you just play the root note?" Why don't *you* just fuck off? I don't like it when people do that. I wouldn't dream of telling somebody else what to play, and I don't like it when people do it to me, you see. I know that guitarists are the worst for it in the world with bass players. And I find that annoying, that bass players go [in dull, passive voice], "Oh. Okay. I'll just play the root note." I'm not like that. That's probably a bit of ego. Or "pride," if you like, either way you look at it.

Well, you are aware, aren't you, that people look to you for a certain style on the bass?

Well, no. I mean, aahh, I don't think they look to *me*. It's like, Bernard had a particular style the way he played; [keyboardist] Gillian [Gilbert] had a style; [drummer] Stephen [Morris] had a style. The reason we were together as a group, to my mind, was because we all liked each other's styles. What happened towards the end of New Order was that they all went off my style of playing. Which is perfectly . . . It's only taste, isn't it? That's what happens with groups anyway. [Belches.] But you know, that is why groups are together. I may as well just be in a solo band if I don't like what Pottsy is playing and if I have to tell Pottsy what to play all the time. Pottsy may as well not be in the group if anyone can do it. The thing I like about Pottsy is he brings in chemistry. He brings in something extra.

Do you think you could handle being a solo artist and doing it all yourself?

No, because I actually tried that with Revenge on my own, at the start. What happens was, you sit there on the first day and get a good riff going, and you go, "That's good, innit?" [Looks around.] "Fookin' 'ell, nobody there!" [Laughs.] What's the point of doing it if there's nobody there? If there's nobody there to share it with you, nobody to enjoy the other bits of this wonderful business that we're in or whatever, if there's nobody to enjoy it with, then why do it?

Well, you have the Thomas Dolbys, who used to do everything himself before—

Yeah, but I'm not damning them for what they do, I'm just saying that, for my personality, it doesn't appeal. It doesn't appeal at all. I like to share. I like to be in a group of people, working.

You did mention that producers had told you that your style didn't go well with guitar because it produced two melodies.

Uh, no. It wasn't guitar, it was things, you know . . . The thing I liked about New Order was that there were layers to it. You could listen to the bass for a melody, or you could listen to the vocals for a melody. It was like a texture. That's what I liked about it. Producers would say, "Hey, man, you can't have a hit if you play something different from the vocal line at the same time!" But that's not what New Order was about.

[Kitchen is suddenly flooded with sound of upper-register bass from hall.]

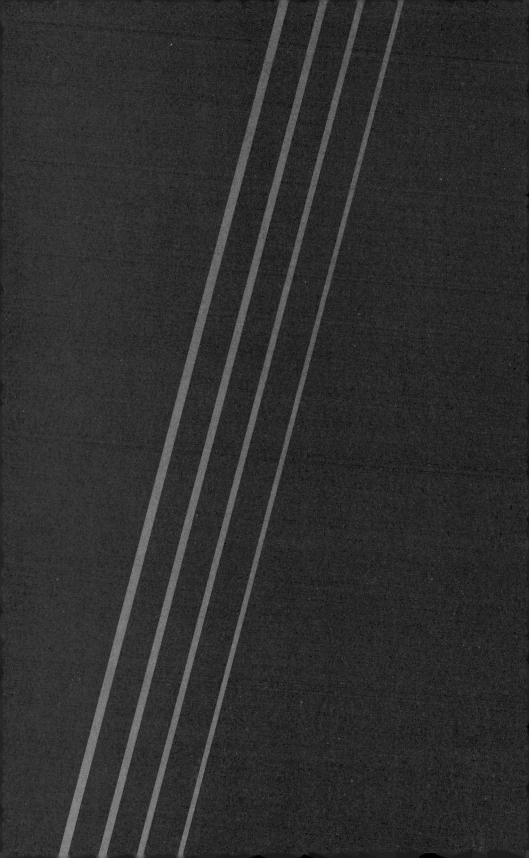

Chapter Eight
Don't Be a Hero

We're hearing the bass right now, right, and not the guitar?

Yeah. That's the bass. That's the other bass player.

The other *bass player*?

He plays bass because I can't play and sing at the same time. [Laughs.]

What, are you switching off parts, or—

No. I play the lead bits of bass, and he plays the bits of bass while I'm singing because I can't play and sing at the same time. I'm fuckin' hopeless, aren't I? [Laughs.] As my mother said, I couldn't hold a tune in a bucket. [In *Monty Python*esque charwoman voice.] "'Ow you stand up there, our Peach, and do that is beyond me because you can't 'old a tune in a bucket." That's what she says to me.

It doesn't bother you, though? I mean, look at Sting, who sings, plays, and dances in three different time signatures.

I don't see beauty in that.

Really? Just talking in terms of efficiency, let's say? Not needing a second bassist?

It's not in the realm of my comprehension. I can't sing and play at the same time. I can't tune up. I don't know what the notes are on the guitar. If someone said, "Play an A, or I'm going to shoot you," I'd just say, "Well, I know the open A, but I don't know any others, so you may as well shoot." I'm not a musician's musician. I know I can play; I can write, and I create songs. I enjoy that, and I do that, I think, quite well, but I'm not one of these [plays blistering air bass for several seconds].

So what interests you about being a musician?

Because I'm good at it, and it moves people, and it moves me. My songs move me. "Atmosphere" [Substance]. "Love Will Tear Us Apart" [Substance]. "Age of Consent" [Power, Corruption, and Lies]. "Shine," for instance. Those are songs that move me. I think, "Fuckin' 'ell, did *I* do that? Wow. I'm *very* pleased." It moves me, and that's it. And I'm quite good at it. Under pressure, I can usually pull it off.

So reading through all these clips, it looked as though people were sort of writing you off for a while. If you didn't . . . I mean, would you always play music, even if, say, there wasn't a market for it?

Yeah. I went through a period, obviously, with Joy Division, where no one bought the music. And I went through a period with New Order where no one bought the music, and I went through a period with Revenge where no one bought the music, and we could barely survive. Now I'm quite comfortable, and I'm okay, and I can survive without it quite well. The thing is, the successful part of it is when you make a record and somebody gives you that and goes, "Well, there's your record that you made," and you go, "Fuckin' 'ell, that is the best thing in the world!" Whether anybody *else* likes it is a bonus, a complete and utter bonus. To my mind, if the record wasn't a hit, I could be just as happy with it.

Would you mind explaining that a little? How you could be happy without selling records? How did you get to that point?

Well, I've never felt success was the be-all and end-all of music anyway. Chart success, I mean. In England, we would release records that had no chance of making it into the charts. "Blue Monday" had no chance of making it to the charts because they didn't count twelve-inches in the chart.

That's a good point, but on the other hand, the twelve-inch became the standard format for dance singles after "Blue Monday."

Yeah, which was fine; yeah. Great. *Then* they had a twelve-inch chart, but it was too late for us. [Laughs.] You know what I mean?

So being a trailblazer hasn't really benefited you?

Well, no. I mean, I think it's just about doing things that appeal to you. I don't like being told what to do. I told you that before. The thing is, I've been spoiled in my musical career by having a manager who said, "If you don't wanna do it, don't do it." The record company would say [in nasal American accent], "We gotta do this interview!" And he'd go [in deep, thuggish voice], "Fook off. He's *told* you. He don't wanna do it. That's *it.*" And the record company is saying, "Gee, man, doncha realize we're not gonna sell records in Ethiopia if you don't do this fuckin' interview? Doncha fuckin' *realize?*"

It was a different way of working, and luckily we had a manager that was on our wavelength. Because we were an independent record company, and we had a fifty-fifty deal. If *they* made a dollar, *we* made a dollar. How many bands make the same as the record company?

Zip.

Right. We still do. Right? So we could survive by selling much less records than any other band. We could sell ten thousand records and get ten thousand pounds in England, while other bands had to sell two hundred fifty thousand records to get ten thousand pounds. So they have to play the game. They have to do this, and they have to do that. We were spoiled, or lucky, whichever way you look at it.

Was that something you fell into by accident?

No, no. It was a deal our manager hammered out with the guy who was our friend who did the record. These two guys were sitting around, and one said, "Well, I manage a band. Do you want to put a record out by them?" And the guy says, "Yeah, all right. I've never done it before, but I'll start a record label, and we'll put some records out." It's just all about that, and the punk thing, timing, the look. It's a fascinating, absolutely wonderful story, which is amazing to me. Even I . . . When I sit there and think about the things that we achieved and the way we pulled it off, it amazes me even. It's like, "Fuckin' 'ell!"

[Three cooks enter the tiny kitchen and begin tossing pots and pans around just as sound check kicks into high gear.]

Since that is an amazing story, is the story finished for New Order?

I have no idea. The thing was that after the business side of New Order was so horrible and fucked up because the deal we'd made . . . That's a perfect example of how it can work your way for a little while and give you more money, enable you to be pure, keep your artistic integrity. But then when the business side starts to go wrong when you're supporting it, it can crumble your music. And what happened was that none of us gave a fuck about New Order or the music because we were so pissed off with the business side of it. [Raises voice to be heard over all the noise.] So the business side of it effectively killed the group in the end!

[Shouting.] You were pissed off with the business side?!

It went bankrupt, didn't it? The record company went bankrupt, owing six and a half million. So then we had to sign to a proper record label. We'd never done that. We'd had the luxury of seventeen years of being able to do exactly what we wanted. And we carried on that way because we were an established group. They can't come along to an established group and say, "We want you to do this or that on this song." Fuck off!

You're with a pretty darn established record company now, though, aren't you?

Mmm-hmm. And they're showing me a lot of respect, yeah. It works very well. I can do whatever I want to do, more or less. At forty-one, you know the score, don't you? If I'm gonna sit in Bali or something, on the beach, not supporting a record album, chances are it'll probably do all right, but if I'm lazy, well then, it'll just dwindle away. Common sense tells you that, if you want it to be a success, you have to work at it. The thing is, there are ways and means that I use. I've had enough experience to know what I want to do and what I don't want to do. If someone calls

me and says, "We want you to do a record store signing," I hate that [oven door slams, obliterating word]. I won't do it. We tried it once in New Order; didn't like it, so I don't do them.

Why? What's the problem with signing records?

I find them embarrassing. I don't like them! I'd hate it if nobody turned up. If there's a record signing and nobody came, I'd die of embarrassment. I'd rather not take the chance. [Laughs.] You know?

[The tour manager marches into the kitchen, points to his watch, and departs, leaving the door wide open. The sound check comes roaring in like a tsunami, so I shove the tape recorder toward Hook. I apparently do it a little too vigorously because he flinches and raises his eyebrows.]

Oops. Sorry.

That's okay.

It seems like you're kind of in the wrong business then, because in this business you're supposed to thrive on that sort of thing. The accolades, the publicity, the photo ops. That's your bread and butter, I thought.

I fail to see how a photo op can be your bread and butter. Surely people appreciating your music is your bread and butter.

Well, there's that old adage—

See, it all comes down to . . . See, I love Iggy Pop, but if I see he's going to have a record signing somewhere, that doesn't interest me. I wouldn't go.

You wouldn't go?

No.

To meet Iggy! To see him in person! To shake his hand!

No. I wouldn't like that. I've been offered the chance to meet Iggy, and I wouldn't go. My mate was his tour manager, and he said, "Come and meet him," and I said, "No. *Fuck* no. What if I meet him, and he's an asshole? I'll never be able to play his records again!" [Laughs.] Never meet your heroes. You should *never* meet your heroes.

Never meet your heroes?

Lots of people have said that. What, you've never heard someone say that?

I think so. Well, why— Why give an interview then?

Well, I don't mind because you're a bass magazine. I like talking about bass. I like it. I don't mind doing interviews. Not particularly.

So what happens when the eighteen-year-old kid who's just started playing the bass comes up to you on the street and says, "You're my god"? He wants to shake your hand and all that. What do you do? Punch him out?

No, of course not! Don't be daft. I would never do something like that. Don't-don't be daft. I'd say, "All right, okay, fine." [Laughs.] If he hung around me long enough, he'd find out I was just a normal Joe most of the time, you know what I mean? Everybody's normal. We all have to go to the toilet; we all have to eat. We all have problems. If he actually hung around me long enough, he'd find that out. I'd be demystified, wouldn't I?

[Tour manager storms into kitchen again.]

Tour Manager: [Shouts.] Look, really, we have to go no later than 6:30!

Okay! Well, jeez, I guess we have enough then!

[The tour manager doesn't leave this time. He folds his arms and stands beside Hook, glaring at me. I begin to gather up my notes and things. Hook rises and then sits down again and continues talking.]

It's very interesting. It's interesting. I mean, you know, it's a very difficult thing, isn't it? I was very fortunate to be in a very unique band that was led by very unique people: Tony Wilson with Factory Records; Rob Gretton, the manager of New Order and the manager of Joy Division; Bernard; Stephen; Gillian. We all together made the whole thing completely different. I'm very glad about that, and to be honest with you, I don't think I could be in a normal group. I couldn't do that. I'm very happy the way it turned out. We were very lucky in that, because we made decent music, we could get away with it. We got away without doing interviews for three years, four years, not one interview. People now tell me, "Man, you've *gotta* go on the radio; you *gotta* phone the programmer," and I'm like, "No, I got away without fuckin' doing that, and I *still* had people packed in to see our gigs." It should be your music, not for your fuckin' talk on the radio. That's what annoys me about when people say, "You've got to go into radio stations," because you don't have to. If your music's good, and they see that the way you're doing it is pure, I think people appreciate that. You've got to treat people the way that you'd like to be treated, I think.

[Standing up.] *Was that why your "no interview" policy worked for you and didn't work for, say, the Knack?*

[Stands up.] I have no idea. I mean, the Knack didn't do very good music, did they? Did they? You know what I mean? [Laughs.] I mean, I remember seeing this kid, he was the drummer with Gun Club, and he said to me, he said, "I've been alone with you in my bedroom fuckin' *loads* of times!" And that's what it's about. When I put an Iggy record on, it's just me and his music. It enhances my life. I don't want to meet Iggy. I don't want to see him or even hear particularly what he's got to say. It's the music that drives you, and that's the thing that turns you on. It's not about him, not what he fuckin' wears. I don't wanna know anything about him. It's just the music. That's the way I perceived it and why New Order acted the way they did.

It was no different . . . Me and Bernard were exactly the same way. We didn't need all that hoo-hah and all that. The great thing about being at, playing a gig, like we did the last New Order tour, twenty-five thousand people, and nobody knew what I looked like. And people said to me, "You walked round the *audience?*" Well, nobody knows what the fuck you look like! I went out and walked around in twenty-five thousand people, and three people recognized me. And that wasn't a big thing. It doesn't bother me. I don't care! I prefer it that way. I don't think that you have to be a face, and you don't have to tour. You can just make music. People make music that moves me all the time, and I don't even know who they are. It's just that music is a gift someone gives you that you put to use in your own life. It's the soundtrack to your own movie—isn't it?—starring *you.* [Laughs.]

Perfect.

Okay.

Thank you very much.

You're welcome.

Hook left the kitchen and went right to the stage, where he strapped on a bass and launched into "What Do You Want from Me?", the single from *Music for Pleasure.* As I packed my bag, one of the cooks turned to me and grabbed the top of his head, squawking, "You guys were doing an *interview?* Shit, man, I'm sorry! I thought you were just having a conversation!" I went into the lobby and listened to the second bassist filling in while Hook sang. He did it so deftly, and the instruments' tones were so well matched that I couldn't tell when one bass left off and the other picked up.

This was, without a doubt, the most difficult interview I'd ever done, not only because of my humiliation and barely contained rage but because the tape itself was almost impossible to transcribe. Hook's accent and tendency to mutter would have made him hard for me to understand even without the noise from the cooks and the sound check. I had to listen to some passages twenty times before getting them. What I rendered above as "the hi-hat's a bit quiet, Martin," sounded in actuality like "theeyai yatsbi kwaa, Maah'n," all smeared together into a long burst of sound. The band name Inspiral Carpets, as another example, eluded me for years because I'd heard it as either "Sparrow Compass" or "Spy Hole Corpus." It wasn't until I got on the Internet that I was able to find a web page for Inspiral Carpets, a Manchester-based group. Hook also spoke very quickly; even though the interview lasted only twenty-six minutes, I ended up with about seven thousand

words in my transcription, nearly twice as much material as I would've gotten from the average interviewee.

As the perfect capper to the situation, Mr. Hook possessed an inexhaustible supply of intestinal gas, which he vented at ninety-second intervals. Between these eruptions, he unself-consciously cleaned his nostrils with his fingers and deposited the findings on his socks. An article I'd read as part of my worthless preparation claimed that he'd urinated into a mug during one interview and tried to make someone drink it, so while we were together, I kept an eye on his socks and devised procedures for getting past him to the door.

It was months before I could even think of New Order without flashing back to that kitchen. When I finally started playing their CDs again, I was horrified to discover that "Vanishing Point" *(Technique)*, "Regret" *(Republic)*, and "Blue Monday" *(Power, Corruption, and Lies)* had become my new favorite songs.

Part Three
Jerry Casale

February 18, 1997

Chapter Nine

Botulism, the Bass, and the Blues

I had first seen Devo in 1981 and had been a big fan ever since. I was in my college dorm late one night, nodding off in the lounge during a rerun of *Saturday Night Live,* when I was roused by five guys in yellow hazmat suits doing a demented version of the Rolling Stones' "(I Can't Get No) Satisfaction." I'd literally never heard anything like it. An apostle of Led Zeppelin and Yes at the time, I was still so inspired that I practiced on my bass the next morning until my fingers were splotched with blood blisters under the calluses. I also went out and hit all the guitar stores in town, looking in vain for a Gibson Ripper I could saw into a teardrop shape just like the one Jerry Casale had. I was smitten. He was hip; he was left-handed; and his bass lines were choppy and weird, not at all like the prog or hard rock bass I was trying to master.

Founded in 1972 by art students Jerry Casale and Mark Mothersbaugh, Devo is probably the most famous band to come out of Akron, Ohio. Even though I'd been listening to them for sixteen years, it wasn't until I did research for this 1997 interview that I became aware of what the name "Devo" meant. Essentially, it expressed a theory that modern technology was causing the human race to *de*volve instead of to *e*volve. The costumes the group had worn—the hazmat suits, the flower pot headgear and leather jackets, the plastic Clark Kent wigs and industrial-military uniforms—had been a visual representation of the concept, but I hadn't known this because I'd only been into the music, especially that amazing debut LP *Q: Are We Not Men? A: We Are Devo!* That record was the one I liked most because it retained electric bass and guitar. Although their later work was more keyboard heavy, they were still able to produce timeless classics like "Whip It" *(Freedom of Choice)* and "Jerkin' Back 'n Forth" *(New Traditionalists)*, songs that twenty years later continue to be "alternative" radio mainstays.

Devo was one of the first new wave bands to achieve great commercial success, I discovered. Rock music guides usually credit them with defining both the eighties' synth sound and the eighties' pop-star cynicism, some writers even accusing them of nihilism, which was laughable. It was clear that Devo was very angry, but to me, anger connotes a deep sense of caring, the exact opposite of nihilism. That interpretation seemed confirmed by Jerry Casale's periodic announcement that Devo had been rock's most misunderstood band. It was easy to see why people got the wrong idea, what with the group's ever-changing, cheesy, futuristically retro look and many alter egos. They called themselves Spud Boys; they were occasionally fronted by a hideous creature called Booji Boy; there was a General Boy in there too, spouting long-winded warnings about encroaching devolution. Every critic had his or her own rendition of what Devo was saying, one of the dangers of being a band with a message.

Pioneers of what grew into the wildly popular genre of industrial music, Devo inexplicably lost their creative edge. Their sound began to suffer in comparison with newer, more innovative electronic outfits, such as Depeche Mode, and each of their records became a little slicker and blander than the last, as if aimed at the very lowest common denominator they'd once railed against. After breaking up and reforming in the late eighties, they finally called it quits in 1991. Mark Mothersbaugh established Mutato Muzika, a production company based in Los Angeles, and segued into soundtracks. Primed by Devo's early experiments in visual media, Jerry Casale went on to direct music videos and television commercials.

I contacted Casale through Mutato, leaving my name and number with a very businesslike woman. Jerry immediately returned my call and suggested that we meet at a restaurant in Santa Monica. He was even more businesslike than the receptionist, almost to the point of indifference. His lack of emotion made me wonder if he'd somehow become the robot he'd pretended to be in Devo's shows. Or maybe, I told myself, *he hadn't been pretending.* The day we were supposed to get together, he phoned again and said that his girlfriend was sick with food poisoning. I thought he was going to cancel, but he casually invited me to his home instead, where he'd talk while he tended to her. I was greatly tempted to accept because I knew it was the chance of a lifetime. How often is a writer allowed to observe something like *that?* I pictured an opulent beachfront, a moaning couch-bound model or actress, full buckets, and Casale with his sleeves rolled up and his dark glasses flashing as he wrung out washcloths and wielded sponges. In the end, unnerved by his detachment, I totally chickened out and—hating myself—rescheduled for the next day.

The restaurant was very upscale, with a large rear patio and clouds of hovering waiters. In my T-shirt and jeans, I was not just out of place but caused the staff actual pain. They all averted their eyes, the other patrons wincing discreetly as I was shown to a table. Casale arrived a few minutes late, outfitted in black from head to toe. He had a bad cold, he said, which was not what I wanted to hear. Illness usually means a cruddy interview, but he was talkative, if cheerfully remote, with the utterly sealed off quality of a veteran homicide detective. He declared that lunch was on him and bought me a tiger prawn pizza, ordering prosciutto and a basket of *pommes frites* for himself. We went over a few current events and then discussed being left-handed bassists in a world of righties. Though a very pleasant lunch date in most ways, he had the one mannerism that always throws me into a gibbering panic: He'd stop talking for a few seconds, and when I'd try to say something, he'd start up again, plowing right ahead as if I didn't exist.

I decided that I was losing valuable material, so I fumbled my recorder out during one of his remarks. I knew I'd done it too abruptly, but I was tormented by a gnawing urge to flee. The waiters would simply *not* back off; my head was being scorched by a nearby gas heater; and the buttery, fishy pizza was so rich I was nauseated after the first bite. Also, I could tell that I was blabbering incontinently. Starting the interview was the only way to shut me up.

Okay, you were saying? About playing upside down?

Because of that, it really didn't matter. Because I could do things other people couldn't do, and they could do things, some things, I couldn't do, but it made me create some more interesting patterns.

When you started out, you learned on a right-handed instrument?

Yeah. When I first started out in blue-collar Ohio in 1970, believe me, I never heard *anything* about a left-handed bass, so I learned to play upside down. When I finally got ahold of a left-handed bass, I'd played it the other way for so long I just couldn't do it as well. I can do certain runs that other people wouldn't do. Certain patterns are easier for me, whereas obviously certain patterns are easier for them, but they're the more typical ones. The patterns I pick sound more bizarre because they aren't something that somebody who played it right would make or do. I think Steinberger will make left-handed instruments if you ask, but by the time I got around to this, it was too late. In my first days, on that Gibson EB-3, I basically slashed up my wrists on the control knobs. People thought that was pretty punk, but it was an accident.

You didn't play any synth bass on the first album, did you?

Everything was real.

Later on you seemed to be doing a lot of stuff on synth. Or did you sort of split it half-and-half between bass and synth?

What would happen was . . . Of course in recording sessions we'd use a lot of synth bass, and I would play those basses or I would program them. By the time it got to *Oh No! It's Devo,* they were programmed bass lines I'd made up. But live, it was a different matter, where we'd find another way to do the songs live, a lot of times. I'd end up playing the Steinberger and do a modified part because it was . . . You know, the programmed bass lines tend to be too regimented and too busy. When you're playing live with real drums again, suddenly there's a lot more air, and there's a lot more push in the beat, so you don't have to play the song as staccato.

But Devo, what it was always about was taking strange influences, eclectic influences, and conceptually putting them together. Even though I probably . . . Aesthetically, my influences were definitely from blues. I grew up listening to the blues. My first cover band when I was sixteen—I had a band called the Satisfied Mind [laughs], and what we did was a bunch

of Rolling Stones covers, which were really covers of, like, Howlin' Wolf, Willie Dixon, John Lee Hooker, you know. All the Stones' first albums were basically blues classics reworked.

And so in addition to the authentic recordings, my influences were, like, Bill Wyman, playing bass lines like on the song "What a Shame" from *The Rolling Stones Now!* Or "King Bee." And I just thought those were just the coolest bass lines because they were inventive. It wasn't like Paul McCartney, who was basically writing a melody line on the bass. It was just counterpointed to the drumbeat, and it was the drums with notes. So it interlocked with Charlie Watts, and suddenly you had this incredible groove that *worked.* Each part worked with the other. Nobody was trying to be a solo virtuoso like Keith Moon. So they left plenty of space. That's the school I came from.

When it got into Devo, then suddenly it was my own aesthetic. It was like we approached it conceptually. I would come up with any part I wanted to come up with, if it fit the idea of the song. So you'd have an idea for a song, and you'd play that way. So I wasn't at that point enamored with a style. I did whatever I had to do to do the bit. So it was coming from my head. There were certainly plenty of bass players who could play more notes than me, but I think I was at least making up original kinds of patterns and inventive, weird lines.

And Devo was all about precision. Suddenly, I got really good—from that R & B background—at playing really precisely, so that people thought it was a machine or a robot sometimes. Especially on those early songs like "Uncontrollable Urge" *[Q: Are We Not Men? A: We Are Devo!],* where there's a bunch of sixteenth notes. I'll-I'll-I'll go play sixteenth notes with the best of the punk bands today. Let them *try* and outdo me. [Laughs.]

The general perception of Devo isn't of-of guys coming from a love of music, especially the blues.

Right. Of course not. That's because we had a sense of humor, and the songs had ironic lyrics that weren't about getting fucked and losing the baby. People tend to see the concepts and the costumes and the graphics and the statements in the magazines and forget that we were really playing music. And we actually got really good at playing music. Live, I think . . . I could show you a lot of articles that corroborate the fact that we were really tight and really exciting live. And Mark was a schooled musician who knew how to play too much, in a way. He was almost too full of clichés, if he didn't watch it, because he could play everything. He played piano since he was about five years old. Bob Mothersbaugh was a very, very good rock and roll guitar player, schooled in the tradition of everything from Keith Richards to Ariel Bender and Captain Beefheart. We used to listen to a lot of Captain Beefheart, all of us, and just loved the way those parts fit together, like on *The Spotlight Kid* and *Clear Spot* and back to *Trout Mask Replica,* the double record.

And we would try to play those things. Some of them were actually too hard for me to play. But we just really admired the bizarre way in which the parts fit together. If you analyze each of the parts, they came from rock and roll and the blues, but the way they fit together was so twisted that nobody recognized it. So Devo was the same way. And I think only later on did people realize we weren't thumbing our noses, and we could play as well as any band could.

You said you were performance artists even though you were never called performance artists.

Right. I think so.

For me, the performance artist's dilemma is [that] you always end up alienating any potential audience. If people don't get it, they're ignorant boobs, and if they say they get it, they're sycophantic boobs. They can't win.

I think as long as you branch out and have new things to say, or as long as you maintain that really delicate balance of connection to the media because the media—or in this sense, in music, the radio programmers—can basically kill you. Within a year, they can basically make you disappear from the marketplace. You don't have a voice anymore. It's done all the time.

Because you're not commercial enough, or because—

Whatever. Or you piss somebody off at a record label. I mean,

come on. It's a small community. It's powerful. Somebody can make a call to somebody else. If [Sony Music Entertainment CEO] Tommy Mattola doesn't like you, you're in deep shit. I mean, when we were coming up, there *was* no alternative music. There *was* no alternative radio. We had to go right for it and still not sell out. And that was an almost impossible task. If it hadn't been for [publisher of rock radio trade magazine *Friday Morning Quarterback*] Kal Rudman down in Florida, "Whip It" would never have been a hit. [Programming consultant] Lee Abrams *hated* us—hated our band, hated our music. Said it would never program on his five hundred AOR [album-oriented rock; i.e., classic rock] stations, whatever he had. He had all those Parallel One Group stations. I mean, this guy . . . All it takes is, like, one Lee Abrams, and you can be dead. At least then.

Not now. The market's fragmented. The market . . . There's many, many markets, and everybody can subsist, which is brilliant. There's more money to be made for everybody because you can have a group that sells ten million records, and nobody else cares about them. They're not a national phenomenon. They don't hold the subconscious fantasies of a big group of people and project them. They just market one tiny little niche in the marketplace. That's what's happening.

We weren't like that. We were loved or hated, and we were kind of in your face, but we weren't punk music stylistically; we were punks attitude-wise, with our . . . More like punk scientists.

[A waiter brings him something called a bloody bull, which he'd ordered after much deliberation.]

Waiter: You asked for a bloody bull, Sir?

Casale: Yeah. Yeah. [To me.] I'm going back on my word here. But this'll help clear up my nose. Temporarily!

Temporarily, yup.

But, um, it was our ideas, our positions, our attachment to eclecticism that made us misunderstood and threatening. It wasn't safety pins in the nose, you know. It wasn't fake rebellion.

OPPOSITE— *Devo, from left: Bob Mothersbaugh, Mark Mothersbaugh, Alan Meyers, Jerry Casale, and Bob Casale*

Chapter Ten
It's a
Beautiful World

Looking through some of those histories of rock music—
They distilled it down to something nasty, didn't they?

Well, they said Devo appealed to a certain stratum of society. "Standing up for geeks and nerds," or something like that. I never felt that. I always thought Devo was something tougher than that, more subtle, so I was wondering: How does it happen that something gets so distorted that way?

Yeah, well, that's the nature of the business. You can only do what you can do, and afterwards, it doesn't really matter what you say. It doesn't matter what your intention is. It doesn't matter what you're projecting. People see what they want to see. There is no doubt about it. And I mean I-I suppose I will never forget as long as I live the huge lesson I learned about the difference between what the artist intends and what happens. Nothing could ever make that boring. Nothing could ever make it less horrible than it was. No amount of time, no amount of, like, rationalization or intellectualization because it's just phenomenal what happens. I could tell you . . . I could still to this day count and name the articles that actually quoted me accurately or didn't come on with an angle and distort everything to the point where I didn't recognize me.

I still remember the best case in point was—there was a famous journalist in England who wrote for *Melody Maker.* I think his name was Alan Jones. And he was basically the king in that era. And he would hold court, and everybody would suck up to him. And he did a, did a perfect whammy on Devo. He came on like he got what we were; he thought we were the best thing out of America. Could he travel with us on the bus? He just thought it was incredible, and he was just very polite and low-key and hung out and was affable. And then the article, which was incredible. Just a massive attack, from the beginning straight down the line. Like, "Mark chirped like a chipmunk. Jerry's head darted fast like a lizard's at my comment." He had us being like all kinds of rodents and reptiles. And then he would go on, and he said, "Devo says when it comes to art, you either eat it or make it. Well, *my mum* made it, and I left it on the *plate,* thank you!" Stuff like that. It just went on like that for four pages in *Melody Maker.*

I just don't understand why writers do that. It's really—

Oh, and here was the headline: "We're the Next Big Thing!" What I *said* was—and it was on the bus—I said, "We're just the next thing." In other words, we're just the next thing that they want to promote. It meant totally the opposite. So he made it like an egotistical statement, that we thought we were, like, incredible.

Artists get accused of cynicism—

[Laughs.] That's a mean word. That's a power word. Sure. Because if a record label executive says something in the press, it's taken to be sanguine, worldly. If a creative person says it, they're the serf outside the castle. They're cynical. "Cynical" is a pejorative term. You're not *allowed* to be cynical. "Cynical" *really* means they were honest, and nobody's allowed to really tell the truth if they want to work.

It seems you can end up being hoist on your own petard without even intending it in the first place.

Absolutely. Absolutely. People decided . . . They wanted to distill us down to something simple and stupid so we weren't threatening. They didn't really want to deal with the content. I mean, a few people did, but when they did, they got pissed off.

Can we talk about that content for a minute? The first sorts of short films you made, I thought they were pretty horrifying.

Good.

I mean, I wasn't angry, but I thought they were horrifying. What were you trying to get across?

Well, *we* were horrified. So we were showing these horrible images of the world as we saw it, and we really did think it was devolving. And I think, if anything, the last seventeen years has proved Devo right. I don't think you could have a Bronco chase unless the world was devolved. I really don't. I just don't think you could have the sort of mindless, moronic discourse about O. J. [Simpson] being acquitted because of race and black people insisting he's being found guilty only because he's black. This is pathetic. This is moronic. We're just talking here about mass stupidity. Forget what color the skin is. Forget it. We're just talking about the inability of the human being—and I don't care what race, and I don't care what economic background—we're talking about the brain not functioning. Period. End. And I really mean that. Because I find most of the idiocy on TV coming from the East Coast Brahmin class. The high-level people, the really educated white people spewing the worst kind of cynicism. I mean *real* cynicism.

The fact that five or six pages of an article can be devoted to lawyers explaining how they used a strategy to get their client out of something and admitting up front, basically, that none of it had anything to do with the truth, and everybody reads it and *admires* them . . . Now, this . . . is phenomenal. This is unbelievable. I hate 'em all. We hated them all then; it's worse now. It's worse now.

Why is it worse now?

I certainly have plenty of ideas why it's worse now. I think the values of Western society were already cracking and in the toilet when we were observing them in the early seventies. And I just think it took a hyperspace drive in that direction. Because it's like any kind of exponentially, geometrically escalating phenomenon in nature. You have way too many people. You have all these people mindlessly breeding, with *lots* of kids. They take drugs. They're on bad diets. The education system's shit because the kind of people that ran the country for twelve years, like Reagan, gutted it. You have absolutely no regard for anything. You put people in that situation, and what do you expect? You have a cauldron of subhumanity. You have the people that rule society cynically just draining and manipulating the hordes like some kind of gladiatorial event. You have people with developmental problems, medical problems, psychological problems, dietary problems, no education. It's-it's-it's a *horror* show. It's a *horror* show. And you have the people who could do something about it, who in the past did do something about it, turning their backs because they got their gated communities. So it's "Fuck you!"

Well, if people give up, do they have complicity in perpetuating the problems?

Well, they should do something about it. Maybe they shouldn't *say* anything about it but just *do* something about it. Try wherever possible to let actions do the talking. It's kind of why I loved *The Unforgiven*. Clint Eastwood film. I think that character as a cipher for the late twentieth century and as a tortured, conflicted human was quite sympathetic. In fact, he's the only kind of character anymore that *is* sympathetic. And you just knew with every moment of him on screen, he just thought, "This planet—" No, not the planet, but the people on it. Because it would be a great planet without the people. But the people on it were just—to him—scum. It was just fantastic. That final scene was incredible.

So how does one prevent oneself from becoming consumed by loathing?

I don't know.

Especially in the entertainment field, where it's easy to—

You have to remain creative. Because when you become consumed, that means you can't even create anymore. You have to remain creative, otherwise you would turn homicidal. Because there's so much evil, so much injustice, so many lies, so many people being hurt every day. If you do nothing about it . . . So many people in power fucking innocent people every moment. It's so oppressive that you have to remain creative, with a sense of humor. I mean, sure, we hated it all. But we were funny. Besides, what else could you be?

Did this idea of things getting worse have anything to do with Devo eventually calling it quits?

Well, the irony of course is that we are what we described. We're part of it. We're part of it. We became less than who we were. You know? In other words, we're like The Band Who Fell to Earth. In the beginning, it was the Three Musketeers, with this vision and this idealism, and then individual personalities and egos and the business and money and . . . It's ridiculous. People read the press and believe what they read about themselves, maybe. I don't know. It's inevitable.

It's unavoidable?

I think so. I really think so.

Is there no going back, though?

Well, you would think that, just like with every natural process of ebb and flow, something builds up, peaks, explodes, takes some time, and you can rebuild. The Phoenix. I don't see any reason why not. I really don't.

Can we look forward to something in the future?

Well, if it was up to me, it would be happening right now.

But it's not up to you.

No. Certainly not up to me.

It's up to everybody.

Yeah. I mean, there are labels that want us to do that right now.

With new material?

With new material. That's the only way. I don't want to be an oldies band. I mean, look: We did things like "Peekaboo!" and "That's Good" [Oh No! It's Devo] and "Penetration in the Centrefold" [The Greatest Misses] and "Blockhead" [Duty Now for the Future] and "Jocko Homo" [Q: Are We Not Men? A: We Are

Devo!], and we had elements of Nine Inch Nails and Prodigy and Chemical Brothers back then. It would be easy—we kind of sired that stuff—it would be easy, using that vocabulary, to write great, big, exciting, new songs that have modern production and things to say. I'm certainly not done yet. I can still play those sixteenth notes really fast.

Would it be easier nowadays to do it?

Yeah.

You were doing things, well, not by hand, but—

Well, we were pioneers, and that means you get scalped. It also means that, in terms of equipment, you're guinea pigs. We were guinea pigs for all the sequencers and for the Fairlight and for everything else. Today, the things we were trying to do, and the multimedia aspects of all the shows we did—they're much more reliable and easy to accomplish for much less money. We never made any money touring. We put it all into some amazing shows.

Did you do that for most of your career?

Yeah. Yeah. We thought we were never going to play live, by the way. In 1974—because we believed in the laser-disk articles we were reading in *Popular Mechanics*—we thought we were going to be like the Three Stooges of the modern world. We thought we were going to make little shorts to introduce new songs and put out laser disks. And the way you would know Devo would be like those half-hour episodes of the Three Stooges. That's what we thought we were going to do. We thought if we did them right, we could just keep doing them. We thought everybody was going to have laser-disk players. But once again, the idiocy of American business and human nature in general . . . Three competing formats, dueling catalogs, the public says, "Fuck you," which they should. It was over.

You said you got really good at performing live. Did you enjoy it?

Yes. There's nothing like performing. There's nothing like performing. You can't go back and fix it.

You enjoy the immediacy of having to do it right the first time?

I sure do. Oh, I sure do. Because something happens. Every time is different, even on the same tour. Anybody can tell you that. I remember in the middle of a tour suddenly getting stage fright after I'd never had it. Bizarre. But any given night, you walk out in front of five, ten, twenty thousand people, and you fight all night long to get the groove, to find the connection, to be at one. And then another night, you walk out and everything goes right, and after three songs, time is suspended; you don't remember; your fingers aren't tired; every single song locks into its right speed; the crowd goes crazy. It's the same set. It's very strange. It's very organic, and it's exhilarating. I mean, when we played Lollapalooza this summer, it was just great.

"Organic" seems like an unusual word coming from you.

Yes, it does!

How can industrial be organic?

Well, I think the end result can be. The process isn't. The end result embodies the human impulse, the creative impulse. And it can feel organic. I mean, certainly there is a lot of music that *is* organic. I'm sure Mariah Carey in the end has a great instrument, her voice, with the dumbest fucking material I've ever heard. Wouldn't it be great to hear her sing a real fucking song?

Absolutely. When's it going to happen?

Never! It's too late. What I mean is, everything is important, and nothing is important. All that counts in the end is what your energy is, really.

What do you think about reviews that said your work became increasingly glossy and straight synthesized dance music?

Well, I think that's partially true. I have the same problem. I think that's what it did. That's what it did. It became all about equipment.

Is there an explanation for this?

Well, it would depend on who you'd ask. But it certainly wasn't my idea. That's all I'll say. [Laughs.] I had this thing in 1983 that I *really* wanted us to do. I wanted us to use the Fairlight only for amazingly nasty, primitive, screaming, animal kinds of sounds. Build them and take a long time to do it, and even though they were on reel, the end result would be frightening. Build sparse sequencer lines and progressions and have everybody play to that. But of course there'd be so much room in there because everything wouldn't be filled up with sixteenth notes. Go back to, like, an "outer-space caveman" idea. Well, that didn't happen, and I sure wish it had.

You're a cofounder of the band, but from what you're saying you sure didn't rule with an iron fist.

No. Somebody likes to put out that image, but I certainly didn't do that. I had a lot to do with overviews and graphics and stage shows and directing the videos and the costumes and statements and all the written material. All that kind of stuff. Sort of a "What's the point of all this?" kind of thing. But musically, it was very democratic. We'd sit around and do things, and the best things got developed. At least in the beginning. In other words, everybody kind of recognized as creative people what was most exciting and what sounded the newest, the freshest, what had the most potential. You find yourself working on something for four or five hours, you know you like it. And that's how it would go. But then it just got like . . . It was almost like we were slaves to the machines or something.

If you did go out tomorrow, what would you do? Would you put on your yellow jumpsuits again?

No. We did that at Lollapalooza ['96], which was great because that's not a place to introduce new material, when you don't have an album or a label. A lot of the kids there thought we were a new band. They'd never heard of us. [Laughs.]

No! Seriously?

Yeah. [Laughs.]

That's so weird. Is that something that bothers you?

No. No. Not really. It's just another audience.

Okay. When you go back to your robotic, jerky presentation of "Satisfaction," is it as fun as it looks?

Yeah. To me it is. I liked it when I made it up, and I like it now. You know, I tried not to do things that I didn't really like.

How important has it been to get mass appeal, as opposed to appealing just to the people who "get it"?

Well, I always thought there was a way to do both. I mean, everybody that I grew up liking in pop music kind of did both. I still think that all that early James Brown stuff is truly amazing. Unbelievable when you listen to those parts and hear the way the music goes together. You see the old videotapes and kine-scopes and films, they're amazing. The same thing with the Beatles, the Rolling Stones, the Who, Bob Dylan in Newport, David Bowie on the *Diamond Dogs* tour. When it's good, it's really good, and that stuff is about as far out as you can get within the realm of popular music. And certainly you can't accuse it of having sounded like the last fifty albums before it. So I do think there is a way to be both original and popular. And the people that do that are always the ones that stay in history because they created something classic.

Overleaf— *Jerry Casale, and Bob Mothersbaugh*

And it's probably much less possible now, with the way the business works today. Certainly with MTV and with the way everything is marketed and packaged, I would hate to think about what would have happened to Devo in the present-day atmosphere. If we'd come from a city like L.A. or New York, where we didn't have three years to work it out in a basement, where nobody cared about us, and everybody laughed at us, it would've come down about the second week that somebody finding out about it would go tell their dad, who works for a record company. We would've gotten signed in 1974 instead of 1978 and would've been disbanded in 1975.

So your success depended on—

Incubation. Incubation and true artistic commitment where there were certainly no rewards, playing that kind of music in Akron, Ohio, making no money. We were a laughingstock. People thought we were just totally bizarre. And sure, we stood for people that were disenfranchised and outsiders. We're for guys like Stephen Hawking, who comes along and says, "Black holes, connected by strings," and people say, "You're out of your mind," and he turns out to be right. [Pauses; laughs wryly; leans forward in chair.]

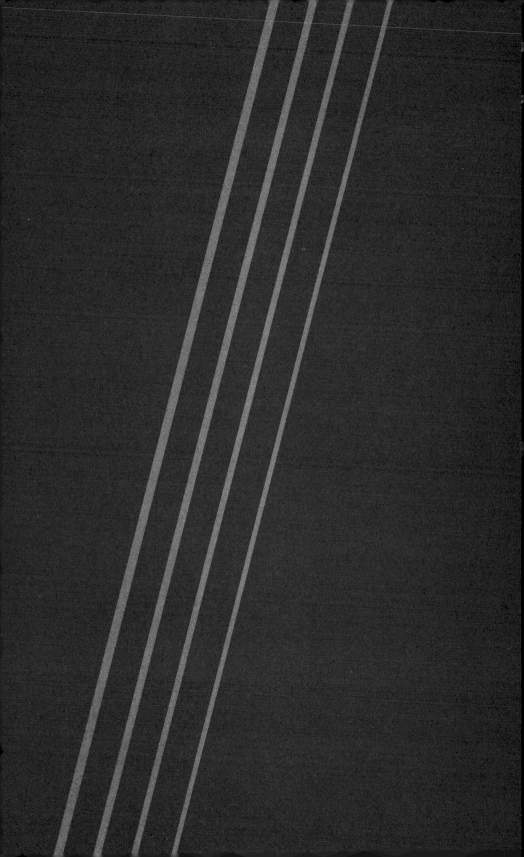

Chapter Eleven
The Pelvis and Positive Thinking

What any of *that* has to do with playing a bass, I'm not sure. But you know what I like about the bass? It's nondivisible. It is the primal root. It is the drums with notes, and it drives the song. Some of my most favorite songs in the history of music are written on the bass and driven by the bass.

Can you give a few examples?

A recent example would've been "New Year's Day," by U2. It's just got the bass riff for all time. I can't imagine being a twelve-year-old kid and not wanting to learn that bass riff immediately. Put that on my record player and learn it.

I forgot to ask before. Why did you pick up the bass in the first place?

Because of the Rolling Stones. I started listening to all those old blues records, and that just kept going. I learned from the people around me. That and the rhythm guitar.

And when did you get into keyboard bass?

Nineteen seventy-nine. The first time I played it in a concert setting was in 1980, in the *Freedom of Choice* tour. Songs like "Girl U Want" and "Whip It" and "Cold War." Songs like that.

So do you have a preference between keyboard bass and bass guitar?

I think nothing feels as good as an electric bass, a stringed instrument, strapped against your body. It's just much more a union of the brain and the pelvis, which is what rock and roll has always been about. Your hand just naturally falls right over your cock. So you just sling your bass right there, and it's kind of masturbatory in the nicest way. People don't mind that you're picking right in front of your dick. In fact, they're turned on by it. There's no other instrument that feels as good. But after that, all the arguments are silly. Whatever the music calls for, what the song calls for, is what's important in the end, for me. And I've heard some amazing synth-bass lines that are very effective and produce visceral responses in the listener. They're just not as much fun to do.

Why did you switch over to bass guitar when you played live?

It just felt better in a live context. It played better to the crowd, and the songs had more power that way. That's why doing new material now, it would be nice to try—regardless of how many parts are playing in the bass end of the music—to make sure that there's a foot in there from the bass guitar. Even if it's just well-chosen notes that aren't necessarily busy. I think it's better to let something tick away in the midrange and then lay down some slower notes off your bass and have the ability to do runs and slides to grease it up.

When you started, there weren't five- and six-string basses. Would you play one now?

I recently directed a video for Mint Condition, and the bass player [Ricky Kinchen] had a very expensive, forty-five-hundred-dollar six-string bass. Amazing. It sounded incredible. Beautiful. Yeah, I'd get into that.

If Devo went out again, what sorts of things would we see?

I think it would be more orchestrated. It would be symphonic anthems with big jungle beats. We'd space out the progressions even further than what's customary in pop music, so you'd have to hear maybe sixteen bars before a line would repeat. And people would just play big chunks of sound. Bob Mothersbaugh would be up on an eight-foot riser, kind of like Slade, with aircraft lights underneath him, and he'd hit some big, bizarre, mutated chord running through a lot of instrumentation. A light would come on over here, and an image would come up in sync with him behind the screen, and the rest of the stage would be dark, and then eight beats later, *boom!* It's Bob Casale wearing a keyboard with another inhuman, screaming sound. Structurally, it would be, instead of a lot of little dinky, pecky sounds, very minimal, big, nasty sounds done in banks, almost like you were doing an orchestra.

Are you making this up as you go along?

No. We've thought about it.

Do you have the freedom, financially, to do more of what you want to do now?

No. I certainly don't, and Mark . . . It's a dichotomy because Mutato is very profitable, so if Devo wasn't, he'd be giving up something profitable to do something unprofitable.

You couldn't do both at the same time?

I don't know. I don't know. The thing is, for me, it doesn't have to be that profitable. I just don't think we should ever get ripped off again the way we got ripped off. We should never make the kinds of publishing deals that we were tricked into. We'd never have the kind of deals with management and promoters that we had in the past. We would know how to maintain 100 percent of our publishing, have masters revert back to us, make fair deals. I mean, when people talk about the music business being onerous, they're not kidding. Nobody, again, is allowed to tell the truth. It isn't just stupid, one-off bands that get ripped off. I mean, big, major bands and big, major artists get ripped off every day. They're lucky to get thirty cents on the dollar. Of course, if you're selling ten million albums, thirty cents on your dollar seems like a hell of a lot. Until you find out ten years down the road how screwed you were. So I just think, naïvely, that deals should be structured so that you get what you deserve from your profits. If you make *them* money, *you* make money. No more "We make them money; we make no money."

After hearing about your experiences and your world-view, how is it that you still have the desire to perform and create?

Well, the way this all started was because I was doing something I loved to do and wanted to do very badly. And I'm certainly not going to stop loving it or stop wanting to do it just because there are a lot of parasitic people surrounding it. I'm not going to give them the satisfaction of destroying my love of creativity. No way. Never.

It means that much to you?

Absolutely. I mean, I love directing music videos.

Is that connected to Mutato Muzika?

No.

Okay. Was that [February 4, 1997] L.A. Times [article on] Mutato accurate?

Well, Mutato has its hands in a lot of things, but whenever they want songs for films, a lot of times they want Devo to write the songs. So I'm involved in songs, not scores, and I'm involved in CD ROMs of course, and I put out a CD ROM based on an old Devo idea called *Adventures of the Smart Patrol.* I wrote, scripted, and directed it. And we did everything at Mutato—produced it there for a company called Inscape. So Mutato is like the Big Brother umbrella. There's a lot of scoring for films, TV, and some commercials. Jingles.

So you're not involved in scoring jingles?

No! [Laughs.] I have no desire to do that.

How did the music video directing come about?

It's something that was part and parcel of Devo. It was like, since we were supposed to be this multimedia video-disk act, I was thinking I was going to direct these things. So when I learned to direct, and I directed our music videos for us from our ideas, it was a natural extension to start directing other people's music videos. And having been a person in a band and signed to a label for a long time, I have a lot of understanding and empathy for the position that the artist is in when I do their video. I know their concerns and their right to be paranoid and

OPPOSITE— *Jerry Casale (left), Mark Mothersbaugh and Bob Mothersbaugh* afraid and not like a lot of what's going on. From being on both sides of the camera, I know how to avoid making anyone look foolish unless they want to look foolish. Which was certainly our intention. We did it on purpose.

Where were the first Devo shorts seen?

The first one eventually got on television. We entered it in the Ann Arbor Film Festival of 1976, and it won a prize for a short. Short subject.

Some of your images are so simple, but they're so ghastly.

Yes.

[Pointing to CD cover.] This "Baby Man" or whatever it is—

"Booji Boy."

Yeah. That really, really bothers me. It's sort of—

Of course. It's mutant and creepy and off-putting. That's the idea. When you have no money, you can use all the kitsch of pop

culture, like masks and products for kids you can get in toy stores. That's what we did.

So much art and music tends toward the negative. Don't you ever feel the desire to have just a celebration of something?

Well, I don't feel we *were* negative. [Pause.] Maybe we were celebrating the negative—like Nero fiddling. You mean do I ever want to do beauty?

Yeah. Something really beautiful.

Well, you know what? It's really hard to do beauty. It's really, really hard. *Really* hard. Because right away, it devolves into sentimentalities and clichés. It is very hard to find an honest expression of beauty that carries the power it's supposed to carry. I think that's the hardest thing in the world to do. Yeah, I'd *love* to do that. That would be incredible. Then you're really taking a risk if you try to do that. That's a *real* risk.

[He looks across the patio and doesn't say anything for almost thirty seconds. When he speaks again, he seems lost in thought, as if he's forgotten all about me.]

Celebration. Declaration. Wallowing in the negative. Sadness. Warrior stuff. Aggressive stuff. That's all relatively easy. But something truly beautiful that isn't sentimental? I would take my hat off to anybody that could do that. Yeah. That'd be great. That's a good idea. The problem is trying to make good on that. Trying to realize it. [Long pause.]

Okay. Um, I always thought "Mongoloid" [Q: Are We Not Men? A: We Are Devo!] was an incredibly poignant song. Was that intentional, that sense of sadness?

Well, what I was trying there was a little bit of what we ended up doing in "Beautiful World" *[New Traditionalists]*, where like in the movie *Bonnie and Clyde* everyone comes in and thinks it's a funny, farcical film, with the banjo music and the bank robbing. "Oh, ha-ha." And then suddenly it gets real hardcore and heavy, and they pull the twist. I think we managed it great in "Beautiful World," but back then, in "Mongoloid," it was like saying "*You're* the mongoloid." It was like, "No, no. You shouldn't make fun of mongoloids because *you're* the mongoloid." So I could see how if someone was in the right mood, especially if they're sensitive or on drugs, would cry listening to "Mongoloid."

On "Satisfaction" [Q: Are We Not Men? A: We Are Devo!], it's hard to tell what's the guitar and what's the bass.

Yeah. What I'm doing is playing backwards to the guitar. Our idea on that was "Let's do Devo reggae," believe it or not. We found out what beat—by listening to a lot of Bob Marley—where the reggae beat is, which is almost a skip. It's a backward kind of thing. We thought that was kind of funny. We thought it was a Jamaican sort of polka or something. We twisted the beat backward on "Satisfaction." The rhythm guitar is just playing the first seven out of every eight, like [sings], *"Da-da-da-da, da-da-dum. Deh-deh-deh-deh, deh-deh-demp."* So he's playing the first seven, and all I do is play a rock and roll version of a reggae line. 'Cause I'm just going [sings] *"Weeew, do-do-do-di-dih, ba-ba-ba-ba-ba-ba-zooo, da-da-da-dih-deh, ba-ba-ba-ba-ba-ba."* So I stop when the beat hits, like [sings], *"ba-ba-ba-bee-buh. Pap!"* So it's like, if you listen to it, it's like some kind of nasty, mechanical, reggae polka. So that's it. It was just an idea.

Had you been listening to much punk?

Oh sure. We had been listening to the Damned and the Ramones and . . . Who else was around that we were listening to? This was before I knew about the Sex Pistols, actually. There were, like, some New York groups. We certainly used a lot of sixteenth notes, like the punk bands, but we just chopped it up differently.

Your bass playing didn't sound much like others' at the time.

It might have been because the bass I was using at the time was a Gibson EB-3 that sounded like a snow goose. I didn't get the Ripper until after that. I was buying these basses only because I have small hands for a bass player. I couldn't play those Fender Jazz basses. So the people from Steinberger came along in New York to one of our rehearsals in 1981, and I put that thing on with the graphite neck. It was so high-tech and

easy to play, and it was bright. With our music then, it was really nice that it had a sort of piano-y brightness. Somewhere
between a keyboard bass and a bass guitar. And it was so easy
to play, and I could stand back and spin it. That was it. Long
after it stopped being hip, I kept playing it. I can play better and
faster on it than on any other bass. I just bought a bunch of them
and had all the control knobs switched over because you don't
want to rip up your wrist and forearm and turn yourself off, and
it's just been the greatest.

And we never played with big amps. Never. We played with
small amps way far away from us, and all we heard was a studio mix through really powerful monitors. It was like we weren't
each alone and couldn't hardly hear the other guys. We heard
what sounded like a recording. And it kept us from losing our
hearing. Also, by the time 1981 rolled around, we were playing
a lot of sequencer lines, so you need a studio-type mix on stage.
You don't want to lose it because the audience is hearing it. On
the other hand, you don't want it to be superloud and lose the
feel and balance of the music.

You did a lot of the synth programming yourself?

Yeah. We made up those bass lines ourselves, and Mark and
I would program them on Roland stuff, early Roland sequencers.
God, I can't remember the model numbers. They were so dinky
and funny looking too. Jim Mothersbaugh taught us how to do
it. Jim was one of the original members of Devo. By the time we
were actually a live unit, he had already gone on to become a
total electronics whiz. He made a homemade set of electronic
drums in 1974 that you can hear on those Rykodisc recordings
called *Hardcore [Devo 1974–1977] Volumes 1 & 2*. Those are all
electronic drums. And he used Remo practice pads and Roland
pickups. By the time '81 rolled around, he was an important guy
at Roland in the development of the company. So we were at
least getting deals on the Rolands, and he would come by and
show us how to use them.

Do you see yourself as a bass player or something much more?

Well, it's kind of funny. I mean, I *am* a bass player, but it's kind of funny describing myself as that because in a way it's the least of what I did. You know what I'm saying? I was much more of a conceptualist and a visual artist and a writer, but I *can* play bass, and I *do* have good rhythm, and I *do* love music, and it did all start with the blues. I was a typical northeastern Ohio blue-collar kid who bought the blues. But it was all about using the brain. I'm just a creative person, and the bass was the instrument I picked and the instrument I love.

I think we'll leave it at that, if that's all right with you.
Okay.

We took Jerry's pictures at the bright green saucer-shaped building on Sunset Boulevard that houses Mutato Muzika. The photographer, a tall, bespectacled Swede named Theo Fridlizius, shot several rolls on a spiral staircase that led to the second-floor lobby. Jerry was dressed in a dark suit similar to the one Dr. Heywood Floyd wore in the film *2001: A Space Odyssey,* a stylish and somehow very funny outfit. When Theo was done with the staircase, he directed us into the lobby and had Jerry crouch in front of a kneeling, life-sized Ronald McDonald statue that had been decked out in a knitted Rastafarian hat and dreadlocks. From the floor, Casale commented that his face would probably end up looking terribly fat. He didn't sound too concerned about it, so for some reason I said, "Well, fat is anger," a line I'd pilfered from the late radio and television shrink David Viscott. Jerry and Theo stared at me for a few seconds and then continued with the shoot.

We moved out to the sun-drenched sidewalk in front of the building, and Theo set up his tripod while blond women speeding by in Beemers honked and yipped "Ow!" from their open windows. Jerry had his Steinberger, a headless composite bass fitted with a swiveling plate, to which the ends of the guitar strap are fixed on the back. I'd never played a Steinberger, so I asked if I could try it out, forgetting that, even though he was a fellow lefty, his strings were set up righty, or

upside down. Of course, I couldn't do anything at all except admire the thing and return it.

"You string it *right*-handed!" I observed.

"We already *discussed* that!" Jerry replied.

He put the bass on and whipped through a few punk-style runs using a pick I gave him. It turned out that he hadn't been kidding; he was indeed as fast and precise as he'd claimed. Theo fired off two or three more rolls of film, and since he's remarkably open-minded for a photographer, he didn't get unhinged when I suggested a pose. I asked Casale what he thought about spinning the bass so it would look in the photo as if he were wearing a propeller at his waist. He obligingly spun the heavy instrument, and Theo took several frames. On the next to last shot, the whirling neck of the bass whacked Jerry's shin so hard that the strings rang. It sounded like a wooden baseball bat hitting a parking meter, a jingling thud-crash, but he didn't even blink.

Part Four
Scott Thunes

October 7, 1996

Chapter Twelve
Background Check

When I moved to southern California in 1993 to be closer to the Los Angeles music scene, I started hearing the name Scott Thunes immediately. Musicians who traveled the alien world of avant-rock insisted that I had to talk to him. "He's the guy," they said, shaking their heads. "He's what it's all about. There's nobody like him." One of Frank Zappa's numerous ex-sidemen, he was an unbelievably gifted bassist who'd turned his back on the industry and walked away in disgust. The rumor was that he didn't even play anymore, which might have been for the best because, as brilliant as he was, he was also an abrasive, difficult, unpredictable weirdo. Stories about him had spread all over the city, campfire tales that opened with "Did you ever hear about the time he . . . ?" What followed was always outrageous, veering into truly frightening.

Jim Roberts originally approved an interview with Thunes, but after Karl Coryat took over as editor of *Bass Player,* I had to clear it with him. Karl told me a new story, the only one I can repeat without much fear of legal action: Scott was talking to a writer at a musical instrument manufacturers' convention. Allegedly. They went to get a drink and found the bar packed, as bars usually are at these gatherings. "This is going to take forever," the writer grumbled. "No, it won't," Thunes said. He stepped into the room, screaming, "GET! OUT! OF! THE! WAY! MOVE IT! MOVE IT! MOOOOOOOOVE IT!" and the crowd parted like the Red Sea.

"So, yeah, see if you can track him down," Karl urged.

My research included contacting musicians and producers who'd dealt with Scott. Most didn't respond. The ones who did get back to me invariably said that his behavior and personality had caused Zappa's awesome 1988 touring band to break up after only four months on the road. Not being a Zappa fan, I'd never heard of the legendary '88 band, but my informants all mentioned it. After the '88 debacle, Thunes had recorded or toured with Frank's sons, Dweezil and Ahmet, as well as the Waterboys, the Vandals, Andy Prieboy, Fear, Wayne Kramer, and several other nonmainstream artists. Of his thirty-plus-record discography, his most high-profile output was the snarling bass line on Frank Zappa's novelty hit "Valley Girl" (Ship Arriving Too Late to Save a Drowning Witch.)

It took two months of investigation to locate Thunes. No one knew or would admit to knowing where he was, only that he'd disappeared from Los Angeles. Former Zappa guitarist Mike Keneally finally acted as go-between and provided me with a phone number. I left a message with the anonymous fellow who answered, and a few days later, Thunes called. Within ten seconds, his abruptness and machine-gun speech seemed to validate the warnings I'd gotten from his associates. "He's a loooonatic," one had said. According to another, "He's not a one-dimensional prick at all. He's an eight-dimensional prick." In the previous weeks, Keneally had lent me more than a dozen CDs and videotapes spotlighting Scott's live performances, and some of the images had made the hair on the back of my neck stand up. Though an incredible virtuoso, a master of improvisation who struck me as a punk-jazz Paul McCartney crossed with progressive rock genius Ray Shulman of Gentle Giant, the man also appeared thoroughly deranged.

I'd been told that he never gave interviews, so I started with a cautious summary of the story I wanted to write, rambling on

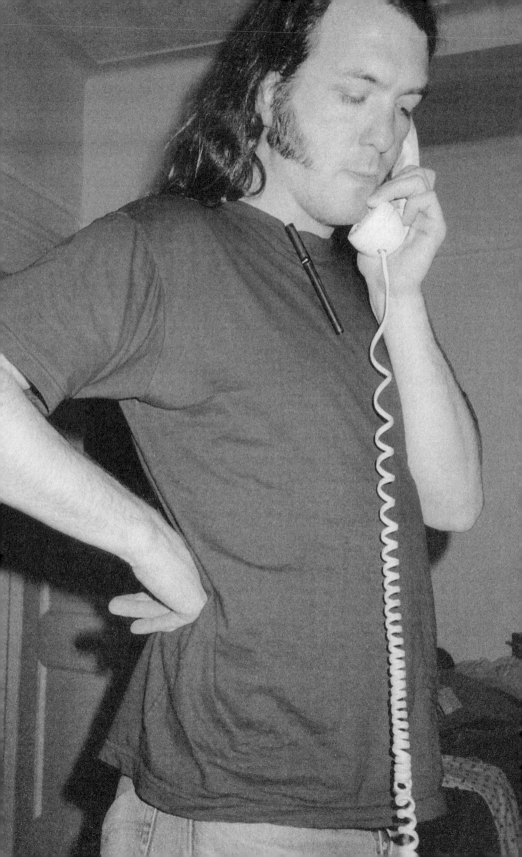

into the silent receiver about respect and fairness. When I petered out, he said, "Darling, I could not *possibly* care less about what you write. It doesn't mean a thing to me. You can write whatever you want." At his request, I spelled my surname, and he grunted, "How'd *that* happen?" Halfway through my explanation that a *Wictor* was a Luxembourgian barrel maker, I remembered Gene Simmons's reaction to my life story. I tried to control myself, but Scott seemed genuinely curious. We ended up going over our respective family histories, and I learned that Thunes, pronounced "TOO-niss," is Norwegian.

After about fifteen minutes, he said that he'd talk with me under two conditions: I'd have to *listen,* and I'd have to come to his house and hang out with him for an afternoon before the interview. I agreed, figuring he was going to use this time to check me out. I asked him what would happen if we couldn't get along, and he said, "Don't worry, you'll hate my guts by the end of it." Since he sounded exactly like the actor Jeremy Piven of Ellen Degeneres's television show, I imagined him calling from a set somewhere, the luscious Joely Fisher draped around his neck.

I arrived in San Rafael on a Saturday afternoon. Scott answered the door with his chin lifted, his eyes squinted almost shut, and his mouth compressed into a lipless pucker. It was the expression of someone in severe gastric pain, a mask he'd don whenever I challenged him over the next few hours. He's a very tall and barrel-chested man with an erect, military bearing, and though his head had been shaved, he'd let the hair on the sides of his ears grow to at least an inch in length, giving him the look of a carousing satyr. His clever, brutish face was vaguely famil-iar, particularly the penetrating blue eyes and slanted brows. By early evening, I'd decided that he was the love child of Michael Keaton and Karl Malden.

He had a beautiful old two-story house, which he shared with his equally beautiful wife, Georgia Morf, and his father-in-law, George Morf. The four of us sat at the kitchen table and made small talk, avoiding the topic of Scott's music career—not a problem for me: I absolutely dreaded asking about it. His employment history seemed to be an unbroken string of failed opportunities, a nightmarish chronicle of swift firings and bitter resignations. At the time he spoke with me in 1996, in fact, he was working as an eight-dollar-an-hour doorman at a San Francisco club called the Paradise Lounge, a development I found almost too appalling to contemplate. Actually, as I sat there and smiled at everybody, I had no idea how to proceed. More than a few of the articles and books about Zappa I'd read referred to "former parking lot attendant Scott Thunes," as if he were a wino Frank had rescued from skid row and slopped into his studio. Zappa loyalists tended to see Thunes as irrelevant or destructive to the composer's legacy, and I'd gathered that Scott was infuriated by this assessment. I knew that the whole situation could turn lethal at any second.

Once we'd taken the considerable tension down a notch, Thunes offered me coffee, his arms folded tightly and his eyes closed. When I accepted, he stood and muttered, "Moo?" I somehow managed to understand that he was asking if I wanted milk in it. Georgia didn't say much, unobtrusively sketching me, I think, on a small pad of paper. Scott eventually announced, "Good. He's comfortable," at which she rose and went to another room. She seemed to have been guarding her husband, her formidable presence a reminder that this was only a trial visit. George was a book scout, so he and I talked about his business for a while. He was delighted to learn that I'd once worked in a used-book store and shared his belief that all secondhand book dealers are insane.

After an hour, Scott and I were left alone. We discussed movies and novels and music. He read aloud from one of his favorite writers, choosing a long passage that described in agonizing detail the process of drinking a soda through a plastic straw. I reciprocated by reading a section from the transcript of my Gene Simmons interview, which I'd sent Thunes because he'd said, "*I* like transcripts," and I'd taken this to mean that he wanted to see my work but wouldn't come right out and ask.

Unfortunately, the package and I had arrived at exactly the same time, so he didn't find out what kind of a writer I was until I was actually sitting in his kitchen, reading him one of my interviews. When I finished, I told him I'd been warned that he was crazy. His face clouded with what looked like bona fide rage, and then he hunched over in his chair and screamed with laughter, hugging his middle. It was extremely hot—midsummer hot—and we were both sweating freely. He had a couple of cold beers, while I alternated between coffee and a cranberry–orange juice mixture. He'd begun calling me "Pookie" almost as soon as I'd walked through the door, and at one point I got quite disoriented, as if I'd been moderately chloroformed. In the conversation, he'd ask if I'd heard of various films or novels or artists; if I hadn't, he'd snap, "Oh. Well, fuck you, then."

We went for a brisk walk, Scott talking constantly. He gave a vagrant some change without breaking stride and then found an Anne Klein designer glasses case on the ground. He passed it to me, saying, "You'd look beautiful in this." A minute later, we ran into a friend of his who immediately stooped, snatched part of a chromed-plastic hubcap out of the gutter, and handed it to me, asking Scott, "Is this what we're supposed to do?"

Thunes and I kept going. As we circled a nearby park and walked along a creek, we debated whether he was an artist or a craftsman, our voices raised to near shouts. He became very mock-pedantic, putting one arm around my shoulders to pull me against his chest and wagging the index finger of his other hand. I had a strange, vivid fantasy of him as Aristotle, complete with beard and white robe, a vision he shattered when he started answering my questions about his past with "Because I'm *crazy!*" Each time he said this, he'd stop dead and gently rub my spine. Twice, he augmented the rubbing with a maniacal hyenalike laugh, his face shoved down close to mine so he could peer into my eyes.

Back at his house, we listened to several CDs of classical music. Georgia sauntered through the dining room and Scott grabbed her, kissing her on the mouth. She lost her balance and fell into his chair, almost knocking it over on top of me. They necked urgently, just two feet away, the chair legs thumping on the wooden floor. Unable to think of anything else to do, I plucked a CD from the tangle of limbs and popped it into the player. I was given more coffee, and when I'd gulped it down, Thunes suddenly granted me permission to return Monday to conduct the formal interview. Five seconds after that, he ushered me to the door, the gut-shot grimace blooming again as he shook my hand.

I presented myself at 12:30 on Monday, but he was out, so George and I had lunch. We were ridiculing Tom Synder when Scott exploded into the kitchen, bellowed, *"No more talk about Tom Snyder!"* and stalked off to change his clothes. He then joined me at the table, looking extremely annoyed.

Okay, my little red light's going.
Very nice. Very nice.
Okay, I know that I . . . You want me to listen, and I promise I will, but first, every story has a beginning, and I'd like you to tell me as much as you think is relevant about your background.
Okay. Uh, my brother and I decided to play guitar when I was eight and he was ten. We both got guitars from Montgomery Ward, with little amplifiers. Little nineteen-dollar jobbies. That's for everything. You've seen that before?
Uh-huh.
Okay. [Mutters.] I know you're *old.* Didn't know *how* old.
Thirty-four.
Yes! That's very important. And after about three months of lessons, I got kid-tired and didn't do it anymore. I was also kind of frustrated because Derek was going to be a drummer, and he decided to play guitar at the last minute. So immediate older brother rivalry: I gave it up. My parents took my guitar and his guitar and sold them and got a better guitar, and that was his career. From that point on, he got better and better guitars, and he got better and better as a guitar player. I followed along as a

kid, watching him play guitar, and after a couple of years, when I was ten, I decided . . . My mom decided that I was going to play the bass because she knew some hippies at the College of Marin, where she was working as the Music Department secretary. Then she bought an instrument from them, and she brought it home. I guess maybe she'd had a conversation with Derek that maybe he needed a bass player, so—

[Phone rings.]
George: [From downstairs.] I'll get it!
Thunes: [Shouts.] *Thank* you!

[To me.] So he'd, ah, have somebody to play with. So I got it and played for a couple of months, and the same thing happened: I got bored. But he did teach me "Batman" and a bunch of Beatles tunes. That was my beginning. By the time I stopped, at around ten and a half, he started hanging out with some friends of his, and they had a band called the Contraband, and they were bass, drums, and guitar. And the two guys he hung out with were brothers. And I went and hung out with them all the time, to the point where I needed to play again. So I was two years younger than Joe, the bass player in the band, but we started being bassheads together. And we had rules: ah, bass all the way up, treble all the way down, had to use your fingers, and you could only play one note at a time.

We were twelve years old, and we had bass rules! I had no idea why we had bass rules, but they were very good. And of course our God was the Ampeg amp, the Transformer model. And from that point on, we had a mutual bass growth pattern. We went to college together; we learned how to play string bass together. Ah, he went off . . . We-we all played jazz. We learned how to play jazz, and then my brother and I decided we had to go to school. So we went to the College of Marin, and I'm fifteen, and I got in early because of discussions between my counselor at school and my mother. And so I spent two years at [the] College of Marin taking nothing but music classes. And most of those were cut because I was in a band. And so I was playing every night—playing jazz, playing jazz-rock, all sorts of stuff that didn't really relate directly to my musical studies.

But the musical studies were secondary to my life anyway. I ended up cutting most of my classes and just hanging out in the music library, which it wasn't until several years later when I actually read a Frank interview that he said he'd done the same thing. Classes don't speak to you. Four-part classical harmony—unless you're a mathematician or really think you're going to be a composer some day—it really *is* dry. And for a fifteen-year-old pot-smoking jazzhead, that's pretty much the exact opposite of what you want to do, is wake up at seven o'clock in the morning and sit in classes all day.

But I loved sitting in the music library. And the music library and the piano class were the two things that changed my life; in that, in piano class, we had to play the [Hungarian pianist-composer Béla] Bartók *Mikrokosmos.* And even the first book, which is all unison, all very simple, at least to almost all audiences, just the melodies, the modal melodies—I'd never heard anything like that before. Even the most outrageous Mahavishnu [Orchestra] stuff didn't affect me as deeply as the simple, strange modes he was working in.

Some of them were just minor scales, but the way he went from note to note just struck a chord—attached itself to my brain stem. And so I went to the college music library and looked up Bartók, and the first piece that I saw that caught my eye was the Concerto for Orchestra. And I got it out of the music library, made a tape of it, and listened to it nonstop for my fifteenth year. I didn't even listen to any other kind of . . . My Mahavishnu records went into the back of the pile. My mom got me a very good version of it, and I got the score, and I studied it like a maniac. I didn't know what to study or how to study it, but I knew that this was something I needed to understand because I'd never heard anything like it before. And I think I listened to it like rock music and not classical music because my mom played piano. She listened to classical music at home. It never did anything to me. She played some [George] Gershwin too and dug all that American sound, but Derek and I were just rock kids.

So when I found Bartók, that was it. Bartók string quartets, Concerto for Orchestra, anything I could get my hands on. And then that grew into all the other guys: [Igor] Stravinsky, [Arnold] Schoenberg, [Alban] Berg, [Anton von] Webern. I became addicted to all that stuff. And at the exact same time, I, uh, somebody . . . This woman brought a, the Devo single of "Mongoloid" and "Jocko Homo" to school. All of us, nine of us, sitting around this turntable in the music library, listening to this song. That was it for jazz. All my friends and I, we played jazz all the time. That was it. Gave it up immediately. Lost all my friends. They all were upset that I'd joined a new wave band. They couldn't understand it. I'd always needed that energy. I'd always searched for it in all the music I was playing but never understood why it wasn't around in Marin County in the early seventies. I don't even remember the rock that was happening here, but it's obviously eminently forgettable.

So back to rock, into new wave, playing in a bunch of bands in San Francisco, getting out of school, parking cars, starting a band with my brother and my friends—the Young Republicans—and then deciding I was going to follow my brother into the conservatory in San Francisco. I wanted to be a conducting major. I'd figured that was going to be my area of expertise. I . . . Like we discussed before, I'd like to be rich and famous for my appreciation of music, and the only, most complete way I could possibly imagine that would be to compose your own pieces and then conduct them. That's got to be the highest high of all, unless you're Frank and you conduct like this. [Stands rigidly upright, moving right arm in stiff, up-down, side-to-side conductor's motions and then sits down.]

I think it's probably just the experience of having the music performed correctly once in your entire life, and it had been your fault you can actually get these people to do it once. *That* was the joy for him.

For me, it would be the experience of hearing and feeling the sounds coming from them. At [the] College of Marin, I actually did conduct a piece of my brother's once. He wrote about five or six pieces for jazz band. The last piece he wrote was for electric violin and solo violin—his girlfriend. And jazz band. Instead of playing bass in the orchestra, in the jazz band, like I normally would have, I asked him if I could conduct it. And I did, and I fucked up really badly. There was one bit that I completely screwed up, and he was very upset with me about it, but instead of getting mad at me, he got mad at the sound guy, who had a bad sound situation, and he and I got into a really bad fight in the music library behind closed doors, in the stacks of scores. We actually almost knocked over a stack of about four hundred scores because we were . . . I was chewing on his finger, and we were bleeding all over the place. It was pretty hairy. That was the last fight we got into. But it was because of this fuckup I had done conducting. That's how I knew I wanted to make up for it by becoming a real good conductor. So I went to the conservatory and I applied, and they said, "We don't take conducting students in the middle of the semester. You're going to have to come in as a string bass major." So I practiced my ass off on the string bass, and I didn't get in.

So I started taking lessons with a private teacher in San Francisco named David Sheinfeld, and then Frank called. I mean, and then Derek went down to Los Angeles, tried to get into Frank's band. He called me up one afternoon and said, "I told Frank you're a really good bass player. He doesn't want me, but you'd better call him up."

So my career from being an eight-year-old to the time Frank and I talked in 1981 was your standard getting-jazz-out-of-my-face, learning classical music as the supreme expression of musical art. Because rock musicians don't know what they're doing. None of them have gone to school to try and figure out what the language is. And that pissed me off more than anything else because reading music is, to me, the most . . . The *second* most fun part about being in music is being able to read

that language. Because I can't speak French; I can't speak German; I can't speak Spanish. I can speak music a little, and to— To go around and see people not knowing that language is a major frustration. I wanted to learn it; my brother wanted to learn it; we went and learned it. And of course the more you learn, the less you know, and that's the frustrating aspect, but Frank found something in me that I didn't know I had. I knew I liked high energy, but I didn't know how I could give it to him. I didn't know why he would want it. What he'd had about him . . . Like [bassist] Arthur Barrow, who at the time when I saw [Frank] in 1980— It seemed to me that he was very happy with that, that form of music. Just getting the notes right. Everything else is secondary. And I couldn't understand, after all the early Zappa stuff I'd heard, why he would want somebody as straight-ahead as Arthur.

But that's what he wanted, and I didn't like it anymore. I stayed away from his music, and next year I'm being called. I go down there and audition, and I'm . . . I go down there with my 1965 [Fender] Jazz Bass, which hasn't been set up for tuning, ever. Never done it. I don't even know if the neck is warped or anything like that. And he said, "You're good enough to record. Let's do some recording." But my bass wasn't intonated, so he sat there on his time and intonated my bass. Twenty-one-year-old schmuck going in there and getting, getting the full, glorious treatment.

Ah, this of course was after me just walking in, and [keyboardist] Tommy Mars is hanging around, and he says, "Sing me a perfect fifth above this note [sings low note]: *laaa.*" I go [sings higher note], *"Laaa!"* I got straight A's in all my ear-training classes. I missed the final, still got an A in the class because that was just something I had. "Uh, major seventh below this note." All that kind of stuff. He went [shrugs and pops out lower lip, raises eyebrows], "Hm. Pretty good," and walked away.

Then we had to record some stuff. I recorded a bunch of stuff. Uh, [Frank] sent me a check; I thought that was going to be it. A week later, he said, "I want you to come down for a week." So I went down and spent four days. He put me up in a hotel, gave me a stack of music, and he said, "You're going to learn *Mo 'n Herb's Vacation* and come back in four days and play it on Thursday." And when I went back on Thursday, he had two other bass players there. And we all had to play it in front of each other. It was one of the worst things that ever happened to me in my entire life. Especially when he . . . Drum machines had just started to hit the high-end market, and he made me play to it faster and faster. And then he made me play it to an arhythmic bit of drum improvisation where he pretty much conducted me through the thing. So I had to play against it. It was pretty good but very, very silly stuff. Major octave displacement, quintuplet during an accelerando? [Sings.] *Da, da, deh, doo, da-di-doo-da-duh.* You know, triple-string, major leaps in a quintuplet, while other rhythm is going on, during an accelerando part of the piece. It was exciting.

I understood Frank's music; I'd been listening to it since I was a kid; I knew what I was in for, but I was not prepared for that exact moment where I actually, strugglingly got through it, and he went [shrugs, pops out lower lip, raises eyebrows], "Hmm. You're good enough to record." And so we sat around and recorded a bunch of stuff. And one of those tracks ended up going out on a record three or four years later. And the rest of it was absolute crap. He made Tommy Mars and I do some improvisation to arhythmic drum-machine parts, and it was pretty hairy. I really have to have a chance to get into something before I can go improvisatorially nuts because I really like to have a basis for communication, and that whole arena left me dry back in my jazz days. I focused on rock and lost that thing. He had to bring it back. I don't know how he knew I had it from those horrible things we recorded that day, but that's what happened.

And he said, "Okay, I'll call you on Sunday." I came home. Sunday passed. Monday passed. Tuesday passed. Wednesday passed. Thursday. Friday. Saturday. It was a really good week-

and-a-half experience of talking to Frank, doing all that stuff, going down there and meeting him, hanging out at his house every day. It was beautiful. But I was just a little boy from San Anselmo who was never gonna get a break, and I wasn't really even looking for a break. This was *already* too much. And I had a gig with my band in Calistoga, which is about sixty miles north. We went back to our hangout. My girlfriend left, drove back; she drove to the house and back in about a minute and a half, easily a mile away. She said, "FRANK called! Wants you to call him collect! *Right now!*" So myself and seven or eight of my pals trekked down to the phone booth at San Anselmo City Hall, and I made my collect call to Frank. He said, "I met this woman, Lisa Popeil, of Popeil family fame. She's an amazing singer, amazing pianist. I need you to come down here and play with her. I want to see what you guys do together."

And she was a maniac. And stuff that he said about her I will not repeat for fear that maybe she would not approve of it. But she probably knows it anyway. And— She *definitely* knows about herself.

And I got hired that day. We went and messed around, and after about six or seven hours, he came out of the studio with his hand extended and said, "Mr. Thunes, would you like a job?" And I said, *"No."* He dropped his hand, and I went, "I'm kidding! I'm kidding!" It was pretty good.

Chapter Thirteen
The '88 Tour,
Part One

So that was nineteen eighty—
That was June or July of 1981. June, I think.
So you got hired that day and went, actually, from San Anselmo all the way down to L.A. again?
Mm-hmm.
Just like the same day? Just hopped in the car and—
No, Monday. I went down Monday. He said, "I want you Monday," and so 7:00—7:00 A.M.—I got a plane ticket. I went down three times. It was pretty good.
Okay. So that puts you up . . . You're now with Frank.
I'm now with Frank in 1981. That's my early career.
You left Frank in 1988.
Eighty-eight. He decided to quit rock in 1982, 1984, and 1988. And that was ever so thankfully my run of tenure. He decided to quit music all the times I was in the band. Mostly it was because he lost money every tour. At least that's what he told me, but I never understood that because I figured that a person as rich as that, you want as many tax breaks as possible, so why wouldn't you want to lose X amount of dollars? That would be your thing. God, *I* would.
Well, can I tell you something?
Sure.

Opposite— *Steve Vai (left), Frank Zappa and Scott Thunes*

I was told by somebody who may or may not know any-
thing . . . The '88 band . . . You were the reason the '88
band broke up.

Of course!

Of course?

Of course. Everybody knows that!

Really?

Everybody except me.

Could you tell me your side of it?

Oh *God!*

If you want.

It's so *long!* It's so long and so arduous, and naming names is
so much *fun,* but I don't know if the person who—

Okay—

He will not approve of it because he has already come up to
me about two or three times, but actually the aftermath is
almost, to me, funnier than what was going on at the time
because at the time I actually did get . . . I went back to being
adolescently suicidal. It was probably the worst time of my life.

But! What happens is, you go out on the road with a bunch
of people, and there's one guy who's the scapegoat. In '81 and
'82, everybody was having a wonderful time except for me
because I'd never been on the road before; I didn't know about
being in an orchestra; I didn't know about hanging out with
people that you didn't agree with and didn't like for long periods of time. I never did a military run, so I don't understand
how to do that. And Tommy Mars was my guy. In 1981 and
1982, he drove me insane. He was the motormouth of the universe; he was an egomaniac *par excellence;* he knew everything; he slept with everybody; he was just . . . He was King
Horse. And he could do no wrong. And him and [percussion-
ist] Ed Mann were pals beyond measure. And they were just
talking constantly, all the time, and it *will* drive you crazy.
Thank God for Walkman. That's all I can say about that.

In '84, it was Alan Zavod, and Alan Zavod we all hated. He
wore the same purple sweatpants every night. He was tall and

lanky and geeky and Australian. Very good composer—I've heard some of his pieces. But he was so bad, Frank actually called him on stage, quite often, "Alan 'Knuckles' Zavod." And he . . . We needed a keyboard player really bad because Tommy was fired, and this guy came in and sight-read *Ship Arriving Too Late to Save a Drowning Witch* really well. He never improved on anything. He learned it to about 70 or 80 or 90 percent. And that was it. Unfortunately, it was also the year of the advent of the [Yamaha] DX7 [keyboard], and Frank only had stock sounds, so it was the thinnest and weirdest, and in some ways ugliest, Zappa band of all time because two DX7s playing at the same time, especially when they're both kind of maladjusted, sounds really gross.

So Alan was our guy because he got solos. I'd never known anyone to get an extended solo. Okay, maybe, you know, other keyboard players *had* gotten theirs, you know, but I wasn't in at that point. To see the band go from a clean, lean, playing music army to having Alan Zavod do "The Volcano" every night was depressing as hell. None of us liked him, and we all gave him tons of shit, and at one point, him and I almost got into a fist-fight, uh, because I said some things to him that were pretty funny. I enjoyed them a lot.

Eighty-eight was my turn, and it was really only my turn because Ed Mann decided for, I think, two specific reasons that it was my turn. My-my nice version, my nice-guy version is— When I joined the band, I didn't know anything about rehearsal schedules and stuff like that. Frank isn't there a lot of the time, especially near the end, where he's got to get a bunch of business done before he leaves. And he gets somebody in the band to be what he calls a "Clonemeister." In '81 and '82, Arthur Barrow did that job. The only reason he wasn't in the band anymore was because he didn't want to go out on the road. He was married and happy. And so he actually got to stay in with the Zappa universe and make some money at the same time, which is a really cool job, especially since he was, I think, the first guy who wasn't actually *in* the band to be Clonemeister. Uh, before he was Clonemeister, I think Ed Mann was. And Ed Mann's a very good musician and knows a lot and would be perfect for it. So Ed's not doing it anymore, and then it's, ah, Arthur's turn.

In '84, Arthur came back. No! No. It was *my* turn. Arthur was doing something else with that German disco producer who did Queen, who did that soundtrack for [the 1984 reissue of Fritz Lang's 1926 silent film] *Metropolis.*

Oh yeah.

Moroder. Can't remember his first name.

Sergio? Giorgio? [It's Giorgio.]

Something like that. And so I was the guy. And we had a lot of fun. Ha, we . . . just enjoyed ourselves. I-I kicked butt; they kicked butt; we did what we needed to do. Um . . . Uh . . . It was great. It was one of the best experiences of my life. I get paid extra. Also, I don't live in Los Angeles, so I'm getting per diem. All the people who live in L.A. don't get per diem, so I'm getting doubly extra money on top of the people who actually live in Los Angeles. And Ed Mann wasn't in the band that year, so there's no pressure.

But in 1988, I'm Clonemeister; he isn't. He's back in the band, and for the first time, he isn't Clonemeister. And I believe, first off, that that was a major source of tension for him because, second-ly, I was very angry most of the time. Uh, every single time I'd been in the band before, downbeat was at *X*. You came before and warmed up. Downbeat was at *X* or *N*. And in 1988, downbeat came anywhere from half an hour after *X* to two or three hours after *X*. Uh, [guitarist-vocalist] Ike Willis was missing in action for a couple of weeks. Uh, [guitarist-vocalist] Ray White disappeared. We had to do auditions. It was a mess. The whole process of rehearsal, which usually takes anywhere from a month and a half to three months, took six months or something. And we some-times only did it two or three times a week instead of five times a week because we were renting this huge soundstage.

The horn players that Frank decided to hire—two of whom had been in the band before: the Fowler brothers [trombonist Bruce and trumpeter-flügelhornist Walt]—they knew the drill. And they threw it away. They showed up a half an hour late with their steaming hot cups of coffee from 7–Eleven and sat around and talked for twenty minutes with Albert Wing, their sax-playing friend that they brought in from another band. And they chatted away and slowly brought out their instruments, and I seethed and fumed on the other side of the bandstand, waiting. And after a while, I yelled and screamed and browbeat and acted like a prima donna fool, and it must have been pretty embarrassing, but I didn't know what else to do. I had bad skills; nobody taught me how to do this; I had to do it on my own. The first year I did it, we had a great time because everybody was on the same wave-length. These guys had . . . Each separate person had their own agenda, and they're all jazz guys, so I'd already been hating jazz guys for so long, this fit right into my pocket. On the other side of that, we've got Ed Mann, [drummer] Chad Wackerman, and [keyboardist-saxophonist-vocalist] Bobby Martin, who would get there at, oh, anywhere from three to five hours earlier because they have to set up all their MIDI programming. And they had tons of it, and they were always there early, early, early, early, early. You couldn't get them to miss a downbeat because they were there. And they'd, you know, stop a half an hour before, go get some brunch, eat, and then they'd be ready.

And at one point, Ed Mann just said, "I'm not going to play while you're conducting. I'm just . . . I'm gonna wait for Frank. I won't deal with you." Only because I was yelling at people that were late. And Marque Coy, who's our monitor mixer, actually kept a log. Frank made him keep a log on who was late because he never had to before, but something had to be done. This was going nowhere fast. And I couldn't . . . I had no discipline for them. I had no whips. And they wouldn't have been any use. They enjoyed watching me have my veins pop out in the middle of my forehead. And so by the time we got out on the road, it was already dead. There was nothing going on amongst any of us. Chad Wackerman and I, who normally had a, a communica-tive relationship, didn't speak at all because of another element that was, could not be foreseen.

Ah, Frank decided to have two buses on the tour, and the two

The '88 band— Front row, from left: Bobby Martin, Scott Thunes, Frank Zappa, Ike Willis, Mike Keneally. Back row, from left: Ed Mann, Chad Wackerman, Kurt McGettrick, Albert Wing, Paul Carman, Bruce Fowler, Walt Fowler.

buses were smoking and nonsmoking. There were very few smokers in the band, and so everybody else went to the non-smoking bus. *Bad* move. But worked out fine for me. Smoking bus: Frank, his bodyguard, his road manager. Those people ended up being on the bus about 10 percent of the time because they would always fly. Mike Keneally, who was even newer in the band than I, didn't smoke but would do anything to be near Frank. Absolutely no problem there. He was on the smoking bus. The Fowler brothers, who stayed up every night, all night long, and played cribbage, taught Mike Keneally how to play cribbage. He got sucked up into their-their game quite easily, and he had a lot of fun. And Kurt McGettrick, sax player, who would sit behind the bus driver with a bottle of wine and a map

and follow our trip. Uh, there are two lounges in the bus, back
and front. Back one has a door. *They* stayed up in the front and
hung out in their secondhand-smoke universe, and *I* got the
whole back lounge to myself. Every night, virtually every night.

On the other bus was everybody else in the band, plus a T-
shirt guy. *Not* a T-shirt guy! Plus a *record company* representa-
tive. We got nine— Oh, and Bob Stone, the recording engineer,
who is ex–air force and a stickler beyond measure. Just . . . I love
him to death, but he's a hardcore character. And we remain
friends to this very day, but very, very difficult to deal with on the
road, very specific. Two guys that talk more than Tommy Mars:
Ike Willis and Albert Wing, sax player. They told me [that] every
night, all night long, Ike Willis would just be up and down the
aisle, hanging out with the different groups of people, talking,
talking, talking. Watching the movie in the front, the movie in
the back, and Ike Willis is bobbing back and forth, just driving
everybody bananas.

Chad and I, who had never had a negative conversation
except for the time when I humorously told him to fuck off, and
he almost in tears said, "Don't talk to me like that." From that
point, I never did. We never had any bad vibes from that
moment on. He decided to agree with the negative energy that
was building up on the other side of the, of the highway while
our bus is cruising mellowly at 4:00 A.M., and I'm sitting in the
back and watching movies and drinking beer and smoking clove
cigarettes and just having a *wonderful* time. Everybody is in the
other bus slowly being driven *mad* with anger, frustration. And
you could imagine what it was like when we'd stop, and people
would come into our bus, and it was mellow, and they would
see me in the back. I mean they . . . I heard things. He . . . Ed
Mann shot a rubber band at my curtain. *That's* how bad it got.
And it got worse from that point on.

But the negative energy of the band fell apart. Almost
exactly a month after we started, there was a band meeting.
And I thought the band meeting was pretty much going to be
about horrible things that had gone on, like being . . . Playing

in Pittsburgh, and our Holiday Inn is ten miles outside of town, so by the time the concert's finished and we get back [purses lips and assumes Betty Boop voice], the kitchen's *closed,* and everybody's *upset* because they *don't* have *anything* to *eat!*

All I knew is you made a sandwich out of the deli tray in the back, and you had food all night. I grab a six-pack and a sandwich, and I'm set. Leave me alone! I don't have anything to do with these guys. I don't have any problem with Frank. *"Don't draw me into your stuff."* So they didn't. They didn't ask me to join into this band meeting. I didn't even know one was happening. I go on stage in Providence, Rhode Island, or Springfield, Massachusetts, I'm not sure which, and—it was Springfield—and I'm on stage, and nobody's there. The assistant road manager comes up and says, "Uh, there's a band meeting in the back." [Pauses; smiles.] Okaaay.

So I go back there. Frank is sitting in a chair—he's *never* in the band room. He's sitting in the chair, and all the guys are milling aboot *[sic]*. I go up to Frank and say, "What's this all about?" He says, "I don't know. What's going on?" I say, "Well, I think I have an idea about what this thing might be about. I have nothing to do with it, but I'm just going to sit and watch because, you know, I'm part of the band." He says, "Okay." Hang out. Three minutes later, the thing settles down. Frank goes, "Okay. What's goin' on?" For one . . . full . . . *minute,* nobody . . . said . . . a . . . *word. No*body. All these people have all these "agendi," none of them said a single word. Finally, Chad Wackerman [earnestly]: "Well . . . There's, um, there's been some talk that the, uh, the horn players feel that the rhythm section isn't supporting them during their solos."

I look around. [Whispers.] How many people are in the rhythm section in this band? There's . . . *Chad* . . . and there's . . . *me.*

Chapter Fourteen
The '88 Tour, Part Two

[Thunes sits still, smiling. He's silent for so long that my voice-actuated tape recorder turns off. Finally, he continues.]

So, inside, boiling; outside, remaining calm. Kurt McGettrick, the tall, thin, baritone sax-, contrabass clarinet-playing, very old, alcoholic cigarette smoker, comes up and says [assumes blaring, dim-witted surfer-dude voice], "Yeah, uh, *Scott*, y' know, when we're playing lines together? It'd be really great if you could come over to, like, my side of the stage? And, y' know, we could play *together*? Y' know, I could be able to *blend* better?"

Okaaaay. Paul Carman, alto sax player. Tie-dyed *T-shirt*–wearing alto sax player. Don't scare me *too* much! He says [assumes whiny, weaselly voice], "Yeah, Scott, it's just . . . You're not, you're not, um . . . We don't feel like you're really playing *behind* us. We feel like you're just going off on some other, on some other tangents while, while we're playing." Which happened to be true. But that, I thought, was part of the idea of getting a bunch of disparate elements on stage and seeing how they blend. This is how *I* play; this is how *you* play. I'm not used to playing behind five horn players a night and having to support them on their solos. I got hired to support Frank. But I'm

---

doing what I do with Frank, with *you.* I'm no problem. This is all background in my mind at the time.

Frank said, "So! Scott! Whattaya think?" Ahhh . . . I should, I should say one little thing: Paul I yelled at earlier that afternoon. Frank wanted to do [Maurice Ravel's] *Boléro,* so while I'm cruising . . . Every city I go to, I always find the music store. That's what I do. I've got five hours to kill, I might as well find the music store and see if there's anything there. Ha, Frank had a little project, he wanted to do the *Boléro,* so I found the sheet music to *Boléro.* At the same time, Mike Keneally is calling his wife, Vivian, desperately attempting to get her to go find one and then fax him a copy. Which he did, and that's the one we ended up using for the arrangement. Mine was for my own personal use, and I'm sitting there looking at it in the hotel lobby, waiting for the bus, and Paul asked me if he could see it. I said, "Fuck off. Get your own." And anybody who knows me at all, they know how to deal with it. Chad would've gone, "Oh, come on! Lemme see it," and I would've handed it to him. But Paul, what were *you* doing the entire time I was out at a music store? I don't want to say because he probably has the same relationship.

But! I have no use for anybody who has no use for me. If the only reason you want to talk to me is to see my sheet music, fuck *off!* No! Absolutely not. I'm not going to play that easygoing, "everybody's mellow" game. I don't need you; you don't need me; don't pretend you do.

So Frank said, "Whattaya think of all this, Scott?" I said, "I am in *shock.* I had no idea this was going on, and I'm very, very upset. I considered to have at least three friends in this band, and not one person has come up to me and said a single thing. I do not know why this is happening to me right now." I-I almost lost it. I'm very upset; I'm in shock; I don't know what to say. Ed Mann said, "Well, Scott—" I said [points finger], *"Wait* a minute! *You!* Don't talk to me. You have a personal agenda with me that has *nothing* to do with this band. I don't want to *hear* what you have to say, and if you say a *single,* 'nother word, I'm leaving this room. *Don't."* He started talking; I picked up my bag, and I left.

I went to the stage. I sat there for about twenty minutes. I have no idea what went on, but Frank came out alone, and he said a couple of things, which were right. You know, "We're all in this together. We're all trying to do the right thing; we're all trying to have a good time here; we're all out on the road together. Some people are a little bit harsher than others, and you're the harshest of them all. You know, I've never met anybody who's so caustic as you, and maybe you wanna think about that." And I said, "You're right," and this whole time I'm bawling my eyes out. I absolutely, just totally broke down, and he said, uh, something to the effect of, "You know, you don't have to cry," and I said, "But I *want* to cry." I mean, I'm crying because these guys are upset, and Arthur Barrow, whose father died while he was on the road, didn't. So I'm obviously some kind of loser. We all have our different levels, okay? Both my parents and my brother were dead at that point; I didn't cry for any of them; I've got things backed up; I'm allowed. I can do anything the fuck I want, especially when it comes to having been in Frank's band for four years; he's never once complained about anything I've ever done. I-I-I'm golden. I can do pretty much anything I want, and this is proof. I'm crying in front of Frank. It was *wonderful.* I said, "But I *want* to cry." I enjoyed myself thoroughly.

Ahhh, but I agreed with him. I said, "Okay, I'll try to mellow out. This is . . . You're absolutely right." I . . . You know, thinking back to yelling at Paul Carman, and it was a stupid thing to do, and that's . . . one of those things that happen. You do those things; sometimes you apologize, and you move on. This time I decided not to apologize. Absolutely no problem. Nobody ever asked me to. From that point on, I was persona non grata. Absolutely 100 percent.

Ah . . . Four people came up to me within the next half hour and said, "I want you to know that I had nothing to do with this. I want you to know that I never agreed with them, about any of the things they said." Mike Keneally was the first; Bobby Martin, Ike Willis, and Albert Wing all came up to me and said

that within a half an hour. Which I thought was very interesting because they didn't say anything to them to keep them from doing it. Did they not know that this was happening? We were, all of us . . . A lot of us were on a bus together. Nobody said anything. So I had resentments immediately about even the people who were supposed to be my friends. Uh, Mike and I ended up hanging out the whole rest of the tour. Best friends. Vivian, his wife, came out, and we went to restaurants every night; it was absolutely no problem.

But! There was a . . . You know, I was alone. I was the only guy who was my friend on that tour. And that lasted for another five months, or however long the tour was. I was alone. Europe: no friends, no band, no nothing. And another time, I got Ed Mann coming up to me in Barcelona, yelling, screaming at me: *"Don't you understand what a privilege it is to play with Frank? How can you ruin his music so intensely, so blindingly, so egomaniacally?"* Constant barrage because I play a lot of lines. I pick a lot of chunks out of the air, and instead of [in Betty Boop voice] "playing the bass," I play Scott Thunes's part in the orchestration of the thing.

I enjoy playing the bass, when I get to do what I want. And of course the whole idea of being a bass player is you don't overplay, and you *play the bass,* all that kind of stuff. Frank has had that his whole life. I don't *do* that; I've *never* done that. You don't ask me to do it if Frank isn't asking me to do it. So I . . . At that particular point, I had to rummage down in my bag and get my headphones out and put them on, and I'm listening to classical music while the face of— Ed Mann's mouth is going [flaps lower jaw] *"Beh-beh-beh-beh-beh."* It was delicious. It was absolutely delicious. I could not understand why a person like that felt he had the right to do what he did.

But! He very strongly felt that and knew that he was right, and there was never any way that the two of us would get together on it. Because all . . . The only thing I could do to make him happy was to stop doing what I did. And I wasn't about to explain to him because he was being pretty negative about it.

Um, you can imagine ten thousand other microscopic little stories. My favorite, and the only one I'm going to tell now, is being on the bus with the Fowler brothers, who were two of the complainants in the Nonsupportive Bass Player–Role Diatribe. Ahhh . . . I came to an uneasy truce with them. And at one point near the end of the tour, when Frank had decided he wasn't going to play anymore because he asked everybody else in the band, "If we go back to the United States and play a bunch of dates, will you go out?" They said, "I won't go out with Scott Thunes again." So when he came up and told me that, I said, "I'll gladly quit." He said, "That's not the problem. The problem is I would have to go back and go into rehearsals again with another bass player." I said, "I don't know what I can say. You know? They don't want me; it's a problem. I'll quit." He said, "That's *not* the problem. I *like* you. I like what you do. I don't have a problem with you, except for all the mistakes you're making."

Because every night when I went on stage, I was surrounded by daggers, so I completely lost concentration. For-for three months straight, I was a wreck, and the music with Frank suffered not only because of my mistakes but because Chad and I weren't communicating. And Frank's only enjoyment in the band was doing guitar solos. And those fell apart. He ended up not doing any. We ended up not doing any sound checks. Instead of three-hour sound checks, we had two songs, and he would get out of there. He could not stand being in the same room with us. And it was because he didn't hear anything. There was no music going on behind him to support him. It was the worst possible combination of events for him. For someone who likes going out on the road, who likes hanging out with musicians, it was really ugly.

My favorite story, my favorite bit of the entire tour—you have to find joy in very many strange places: I'm sitting in my back lounge, Frank's back lounge on the bus, cruising along the Berlin Corridor, maybe. That's the visualization I have. And what's-his-name. [Strikes tabletop several times.] Bruce . . . *Fowler* wants to know why I was such an asshole. I said, "I do

not agree with that assessment. I am *not* an asshole; I am *me.*
You don't have to like me, but I am not going to say that I did
anything wrong because I have not been told by Frank that I did
anything wrong. You guys don't like it, that's fine. I don't wanna
hear a thing, another thing about it."

He said . . . He just got talking about it. He spent another
two or three minutes; I said, *"Shut up!* I don't wanna hear it.
Get out of here!" He wouldn't leave. So I stood up . . . Mike
Keneally and I had been drinking champagne in the back, and
Mike was pretty mellow; he was pretty . . . We were gettin'
pretty drunk. And Bruce Fowler would not shut up. So I stood
up, and I dropped my pants, and I stood with my *cock*—and
balls—three inches in front of his face. He sat there like this
[assumes hangdog expression, head turned to the side as if
holding his breath], cock right here [puts finger next to his
cheek], for thirty seconds, and he got up. But this is a guy who
eats his own boogers. So I don't really worry about most of
the things that happen to this guy. And, ah, and that was it.
They left me alone, from that point on, uh, thankfully. But
nobody ever, *ever* tried to understand my point of view.

At the end of the tour, we were playing in some German
place, near the end of the tour. Eh, Darmstadt. And Frank wanted to do a twelve-tone piece because that's where the Darmstadt School started, which was [Olivier Eugène Prosper
Charles] Messiaen, [Pierre] Boulez, Luigi Nono, Stockhausen, all
those cats sat around and—Bruno Maderna—and they all sat
around and studied Webern. Webern was their God, not
Schoenberg, because Webern was even more serial than even
Schoenberg was, and that's a whole different kind of music.

But! Frank wanted to do a twelve-tone row, so he said, "Find
me the Webern row from the Concerto Opus 24," and I knew it
very well, but I didn't have the score. But I knew how that row
was constructed, so I built a row that has the exact same prop-
erties of mutual . . . It's the same motif, same three-note motif,
four times, with retrograde and inverted transpositions, even
within the row. That's how detailed Webern got with this shit.

So I *built* one, but it was mine. I wrote it on the back of a couple of pieces of music paper, and all my paper was filled, so I had to tear it up, so that my music on the other side was still legible, so I think when I got the pieces back, I could still have them. And I wrote out these rows, and I gave them to a bunch of the musicians, so at any point, Frank could point to them, and we would do automatic twelve-tone music. You know, he even said, "You transpose it up a fifth; you transpose it down a third," that kind of thing. And—

I *didn't* tear up the pieces of paper, *that's* what happened. I wrote them out on separate pieces of paper. On one of the pieces of paper that I had given to Bruce Fowler, he—because I wrote two different rows, something like that, for two different positions—he tore my music paper in half and handed one half to somebody else so they could write up their own riff, something like that. I got mad at him for tearing up my paper, and he thought I was insane. He thought I was absolutely, dramatically *banal* in my humanity. He could not understand why, for any reason, I would be upset. Same night, in a conversation with

him, asking him—ah, *telling* him—"You guys were late every night; that was one of the reasons why I was such an asshole." He said, "We were never late once." He said him and his brother were never late to a rehearsal once. I know for a fact they were late seventy-five times. Every single *time,* they were late. He told me to my face they were never, ever late once. And that was the end of our relationship because you don't lie to me. I may be wrong; I may have my facts incorrect, but I will stand corrected immediately. But you don't blatantly do something like that. Marqueson [Marque Coy] has proof! "Why would you say that to me? There's nobody else in the room! [Laughs.] There's nobody gonna hear you!"

So that was what that tour was like. And the cake thing. It's probably documented somewhere else, but it was just an ugly moment in my life. We played in some city in Austria where they gave us a marzipan cake in the shape of a guitar, and it had all the band members' names in frosting on it. And I showed up, coming out of the bus ten minutes later so I wouldn't have to meet the rush of band members coming out, which happened every night, and somebody had taken a knife and drawn a nice little, you know, inch-deep line through my name written in the frosting. And of course the best thing would have been to stand up and walk away, but I had just had too much, so I took a spoon, and I scooped out Ed Mann's and Chad Wackerman's names.

Now, this is where all, everything, all the fantasyland comes from, is this cake event, where I did something stupid. I played back into their hands. I should not have done it, but I did it, and I didn't enjoy it, but when Frank had to discuss it with me afterwards, saying, "So what's this with the cake?" "Ah, well, they crossed me out." "Well, you know, what'd you do?" [Shamefacedly.] "Well, I scooped their names out." And the look I got from him was one of the most *painful* looks I have *ever* gotten from him. Out of all the clams I've thrown and all the clamps he's had to put down on me, that was the one . . . "I am showing you, Frank, exactly how much of an anus I am. There's noth-

ing worse than what I just did, for me. I can imagine what it feels
like to you." He was one of the most fair people I've ever met.
He understands about that kind of stuff.

So! I got a couple of good licks in, ah, in song later that night.
Frank used it as the basis for the Magic Word in "Illinois Enema
Bandit," and that was pretty much my getting back at the guys,
was him giving me a chance to have my story be told in song,
uh, about how bad these guys were. But unfortunately, at the
very end [when he sings about people needing misery in their
lives, he's] pointing back at me, so, you know, he's not gonna let
me get away scot-free either, no pun intended.

And then there was the laminate. This actually happened
first. We each got a picture laminate, and the laminate story,
which is where all this stuff really started, was before the
cake. Everybody knows about the cake, but nobody knows
about the laminate because that's my own personal property.
I took my laminate off and handed it to the guitar tech every
night so it wasn't dangling in front of me, and sometimes I'd
pop it on my pants, but most of the time just take it off and
leave it there on the tech stand. I came back one night, and
somebody had taken a very sharp object and jabbed my picture about ten times. [Clenches fist and pounds tabletop
viciously ten or twelve times, face all puckered up.]

So I kept it on my person for about a week, and then I
thought the danger zone was over, and I left it there again.
And when I got back that night, my picture had been cut *out*
of my laminate. This was before the cake, okay? I hadn't done
anything to anybody in months.

But! All the guys had turned the crew to their side. Because
I don't hang out with the crew that much. I hang out with the
guitar tech, but, ah, you know, we got thirty people in another bus following us around, bringing up the lights and the
equipment, stuff like that. Some of those people I've known
for several years, and they're my friends, but other people are
just hired for this tour. They don't know dick about me. They
just know about my [in prissy, purse-lipped voice] *"caustic*

sense of *humor.*" That's it. So that was when I went to Frank and said, "I'm freaking out. This is too much. I don't know what to do." And he said . . . [Long pause.]

Go ahead.

I *know!* I'm thinking of the term. I'm trying to think who it was. [Bassist] Jeff Simmons had a term for what they were doing: "playground psychotics." [Frank] ended up making it the name of an album. Um . . . Great! Fine! That doesn't help me. I know they're crazy. I know I'm right. I know I haven't done anything to them in months, at least. That doesn't help. I'm freaking out.

And that was it. The whole rest of the, you know, two and a half months of the tour was just hell, and then it got worse for Frank, and then he gladly broke up the band. There wasn't even a breaking up of the band. There was no band to break up. Everybody in the band didn't want to play with me. That's the breaking up of the band. Blame it on me because of my personality? Excellent! Go for it.

Chapter Fifteen
Entropy

Okay. Take me from '88 to the present.
Mm-hmm.
I know you played with Fear—
That was the most recent thing.
Okay. What did you do between, say, the '88 . . . You did . . . I keep seeing stuff with early nineties dates on it. Does that mean when they were released or when they were—
When they were *re*released. These were rereleased by Rykodisc in this new format twice. All this kind of stuff, all that stuff. In 1988 . . . Nothing past '84 in this [holds up CD of *Guitar*], I don't think. Um . . . In 1986 . . . Well, it was in the four-year hiatus—I moved to New York, and I spent almost a year there, and when I came back to northern California, I was here for about three weeks when Frank called and said, "I'd like you to come down here and help me put Dweezil's first album together." And I said, "Absolutely *not* am I going down to Los Angeles. There's no way I'm going to spend any time—"
Actually, he said, "Come down here and-and I want you to put string bass on the London Symphony Orchestra tapes that I just have finished." And I said, "Fine! I'd love to do that." And, "Why don't you come down here and stay down here for a couple months and work on Dweezil's album," and I said, "Absolutely *not!*" So I went down there with my girlfriend because she said, "Maybe it'll be good for your career." So I

OPPOSITE— *Z, from left: Scott Thunes, Mike Keneally, Ahmet Zappa, Joe Travers, and Dweezil Zappa.*

went down to Los Angeles. It was her decision. She totally rescinded that later on. She completely blamed me for dragging her to Los Angeles a year later. But at that particular time, it was definitely her idea because I-I wouldn't have left this anyway.

But! So I go down there. I spend a couple of months down there. I helped Dweezil put his album together, and that's it. And that's . . . You know, when Chad Wackerman was coming in and doing the stuff, I personally would not have chosen him because it was a more hard rock thing, and Frank wanted . . . It was . . . It . . . At that point, it became his band, supporting Dweezil. I definitely didn't want that idea. But there were no other drummers around, and so we did that, and it worked out for whatever, ah, goodness that was there.

Um, then I was doing some construction down in Los Angeles. And then my friend Ed Berman decided to call me up to come back here and play in a band with him. And once again, my girlfriend said, "You might as well go." She blamed me for that as well and said she had nothing to do with it, that I was *leaving* her, but in actuality she . . . I was going to come up here and make tons of money. I was making anywhere from one to six hundred dollars a night playing in this band. And—

Playing in . . .

Ah, playing in a band that did Motown. It was, ah, four chick singers, four horn players, two keyboard players. Big, big band. And they were very popular. I came up and played with that for a year. Moved back up here in 1987. When that died, Frank called back. *No!* Dweezil said, "We're about to do album number two." So I went back down to Los Angeles and did the second album. Stayed down there for several months. I don't remember . . . *That's* what it was! I moved down there; I ended up living at [former Zappa guitarist] Steve Vai's house in the Valley. He ended up moving into Hollywood, and I stayed there with his friend Marty Schwartz for a year, recording this album in 1987. At the end of that album, I was there for a couple of months, and Frank decided to do '88. So from '88 . . . We did the

'88, and then I stayed in Los Angeles. I remained in Los Angeles, and then for six months I didn't do anything. [Long pause.]

I *guess* I started playing with Dweezil again. *That's* what I did! Immediately I started playing with Dweezil again. Started rehearsing . . . We found this drummer, Josh Freese, and we rehearsed every day. We just had tons of fun, *that's* what happened. Weren't . . . I was getting paid a little. Enough to survive, but just barely. And then I met my wife, my first wife, in Germany and brought her back, married her. All this time I was in Dweezil. Most of the time I wasn't making much money so I started doing temp work. I was doing data entry, answering phones, you know, suit-and-tie stuff. Ten bucks an hour. And I did that and Dweezil for a couple of years, just straight. Just nothing but Dweezil, and then all of a sudden, certain things popped up. I'd do an album here; I'd do this and that. I ended . . . I don't . . .

That whole thing is just a complete blur to me because I was just trying to deal with my wife and trying to deal with Dweezil. Working in the Dweezil band for three hundred dollars a week. I went back and forth between being suicidal because it was so stupid and thanking somebody that I was making money being a musician. I try not to look at it as a, as a downward spiral or an upward spiral or anything. I really enjoyed the music, and I enjoyed hanging out, the three of us—Dweezil, Josh and I—in a room playing his music. It helped me to orchestrate it, telling Josh what to do and all that kind of stuff. I enjoyed it very much.

But! What ended up happening was that we went out on the road, and the first time we went out on the road, it was fun. We went out and did three shows in two weeks. So the whole time we were just hanging out having a really good time. Hanging out with Josh, being buds. And then came back and were about to do another album—I guess this was the fourth one—Josh quit. We spent three months auditioning drummers. We used six or seven on the album. When we went to go tour for that, the drummer that we wanted, Toss Panos, was not available, so they hired this guy.

Eighty-eight all over again, except this time, it was this drummer. And I never wanted another band, but we needed to go out on the road, and he was available. He'd gone to Berklee [College of Music in Boston] and could play and really wanted to be in the band, and Mike Keneally—who's Mr. Nice Guy—says, "Well, this guy can play, and he's a steady musician, and he worships Dweezil's music, so we should get him in the band," not realizing that, knowing that I would hate him anyway, hoping against hope that things, that I would mellow out, or that I'd be able to deal with it, or that this drummer would elevate his spirit and intellect to at least meet the challenge. Failed dramatically. Guy was a *classic* bonehead, and in the middle of that tour, I offered to perform fisticuffs with him because he continued to throw sticks into the audience, which Mike Keneally and I had told him at the very beginning of the tour was not a thing you do. "Do not do it. We don't like it. We don't enjoy it. You're not in a rock band. This is an *anti*rock band."

During the course of being on that three-and-a-half-month tour—or two-and-a-half-month tour—in Europe with Dweezil, it became a rock band. And all my cynical rock grimaces ended up becoming out of place because they actually *were* starting to do things. So after I offered to perform fisticuffs upon this drummer's person, I realized that it wasn't going to mesh very well with the rest of the tour, so I'd never apologized. We had a couple nights off; I got a band meeting together, and I laid open my soul. I apologized profusely to this drummer. I said, "I'm really sorry." He said, "I understand you're saying you're sorry, but I'll never forgive you," and "I've been hurt too much," and "That figures!" And so absolutely no problem, but unfortunately it laid me open to denigration from the rest of the guys, and at one point Dweezil started crying. It got really ugly. He was, I think, emotionally battered from some other thing that was happening in his life, but he was very upset at my lack of sensitivity in a bunch of other areas including that I—

We played in France somewhere, and there's a drum and guitar duet at one point in the show, and everybody usually leaves the stage. I decided to go get my briefcase, come back to the stage, open up my briefcase, put on my headphones—I was listening to [the band] They Might Be Giants, a tape, a compilation tape I'd put together—and started doing a crossword puzzle.

I'd heard this story. Again, garbled. Go ahead.

And that was it. [Dweezil] told me in this band meeting that [he] was not prepared for [me to do] anything else except just to apologize to the guys in the band, that I had caused tension, and to this drummer person, who I had obviously hurt beyond measure, that I was wrong. And I opened myself up to a bunch of other things, and of course Dweezil and Ahmet got into it amongst themselves for certain things. It became a band meeting; it was pretty ugly. And in the Dweezil universe, you don't have a band meeting because everything has to be his way or not at all. It gets really sad if he has to deal with anything tensionful because he's not a band leader, nor will he ever be. And if he thinks he is, he's very bad at it.

But! That's all that happened that one night. He said something else akin to my constant negativity, which obviously is a generalized attitude anyway. If I'm going to be having to deal with this asshole, you're going to have to be dealing with *me* as an asshole as well. That's just the way I am. And there wasn't much else to that particular story. I apologized again, thinking, "This is absolutely beyond my frame of reference. I am supposed to be able to humorously exhibit odd stage patterns to show that the whole concept of being in a rock band is not to perform to the audience but to be musicians. I'm presenting this music to people, I'm getting paid, and that's it. I'm not offering anything to you because you're not offering anything to me. It's all about the leader of the band, and I'm the side guy." That's been happening after . . .

If it weren't for Frank, that would not be my mode of reference, but I'd always played in an orchestra where there's a leader who is the center of attention and I've looked into the audience. I've seen the lack of comprehension of my person. Maybe I *am* the bass player in this arena, but I consider myself

to be my own person. So when I go out there, I stop being Scott Thunes, human being. I'm Robot #65 Bass Machine, in certain arenas. In this one, it definitely worked because I don't like playing behind guitar players. I like playing good music. That's what I do. I play good music. And he was upset, and I offered to quit. I said, "If you ever feel the need to have me be replaced, go right ahead and do it."

So when I got home, I didn't hear hide nor hair from anybody for about three weeks, and Dweezil called me up one day and said [sighs dramatically; grimaces], "It's so *strange!* Um . . . *God,* this is strange."

[Side A of the first tape ends. Thunes has been talking for an hour. I turn the tape over, and he continues.]

"Ah . . . I can't use you anymore because I don't have enough money to have all three of you have your own hotel rooms," which is what happened for, I guess, a week or something after I got into this argument with the drummer. Because we did a trio pair-off: *A* and *B* would stay in a room, and *C* would get his own. The next city, *B* and *C* would pair together, and *A* would get alone. Of course, the first two weeks we were out, I was always paired with somebody. The scheduling got completely fucked up. I'd been talking to Gail [Zappa, Frank's wife], so that's where tension was created in that arena as well.

But! He said, "I can't afford to have separate hotel rooms for you guys. I need somebody nicer in the band. So I've been rehearsing with this guy, and he's really nice, and it's working out fine." I said, "Okay, fine." What else can I say? I'm fired. And, ah . . . He said, "It's just so *strange!*" Um . . . He's never had to really fire anybody before, and he's not a band leader. He's just a kid guitar player with the wherewithal to perform. And that was it. And I didn't hear hide nor hair from anybody. Mike called me three or four days later. Everybody else who was involved in the organization never called me back.

This is '93?

Yeah. Uh . . . I was on retainer. It was the only time I'd ever been on retainer with the Zappas, and they fired me about six months before the end of the year, before the end of the retainer period. And Dweezil said, "Well, just talk to Gail, and she'll set up a . . . You know, you can have a lump sum, or we'll continue on with the weekly payments." And I never called her, figuring they'd just continue on with the weekly payments. The weekly payments *stopped*, and I never heard from them again. But I left with, uh, a chunk of equipment that, at the time it was purchased, equaled the amount of money they owed me, sort of, and so we just left it at that. They never called me back to get the piece of equipment back, and I never called them to get the money. I just let it ride. So that was the end of that.

After Dweezil, within two or three months, Steve Vai called. His sister actually called—his secretary, Pam—and said, "Steve needs you to audition," because Marty, who's my best friend down there, ah, hangs out with Steve all the time. He told Pam, "Why don't you call Scott?" And my name had never popped into Steve's head except as a tenant in his house because, after the '82 tour, we never communicated. There was nothing to communicate about. And so I went and auditioned, and I forgot my bass in the back of Marty's truck. So they had to go and rent a bass for me, and I guess I was good enough. I hadn't even heard any of the music. I went in and just kind of played, and he hired me. So I went out on the road with Steve for two and a half months, and *that* was one of the most hellish experiences of my life. And if I hadn't blocked all of it out, I'd have another three or four tapes of stories because that stuff's even more exciting to me than Frank stories because Frank stories are almost uniformly positive, and Steve's stories are almost uniformly negative for the most amazing reasons. Absolutely beautiful.

But I went out, and I came back and— Oh, during the Dweezil period, at one point, I— *That's* what it was! At the end of the tour, I went out with Dweezil, I talked to my girlfriend or some other people that were around, and they said that the Waterboys were auditioning for a band, and I'd already played on the album several months previous. And I guess it was in January that I played on the album, January or February, and around June or something, when we're out on the road, I get this message. So I decide to stop in New York before I go back to Los Angeles, and I spent a week and a half there auditioning with this band, and I think that confused Dweezil because I . . . He thought I was quitting on him, so there was a combination of me going out and auditioning and not telling anyone in the band where I was going. But, you know, these things come around eventually. He must've known. And of course, you know, he didn't hire anybody; Mike Scott from the Waterboys didn't hire anybody, and he ended up quitting music and going back to Scotland where he recorded solo albums and stuff like that.

But! At the time, I was asking anybody for a gig because it was getting really over with Dweezil. So the Waterboys fell through; Steve Vai was ridiculous but doable. When I got back, I just played on my friends' demos and did some straight gigs. Came up here and did some gigs, and *that's* becoming a blur to me now because I don't remember what I did between the big Steve Vai tour and a bunch of the other things. I delivered records! Once a week, for about two years. And that's . . . That was, you know, five hundred bucks a month. There's . . . My girl-friend was working, and we were surviving, and that was it. And, um, then I decided to play with Fear because Josh Freese had gotten me this demo gig, and I went and did the demo and had a really great time. It was punk, and I said, "Oh my God! This is *exactly* what I've been wanting to do my entire life." Play complicated, hard-edged, fast music that people can actually dance and pogo and freak out to, instead of this analytical hard rock stuff, which only goes to the front of the stage and then stops, energy-wise.

What year was this? Fear.

Ah, that was '93. That was later in '93. As a matter of fact, I was . . . After the demo, I was hoping to go out with Fear instead of Steve. You know, "Please!" You know, "Get it together, Lee [Ving, guitarist and frontman of Fear], and let's go out on the

road." So nothing happened for a long time. A *really* long time, until he finally got some funding, and we started rehearsing. Then he fired his guitar player, and we auditioned for a couple of months, and he hired the guitar player back. We rehearsed for another three or four months, and then we went out on the road for six weeks, and then *that* got ugly. Him and I got into a huge argument within the first three weeks, and I decided to quit about twelve times after that. And there's about twelve or thirteen stories because of that.

But! That didn't last long because him and I were never meant to spend even six minutes in the same room together because he's . . . Well, I don't want to get my ass kicked. I'm not going to say any more about Lee. He's a very, *very* big man—metaphorically and width-wise—and very muscular.

So Fear—
And scary.
So Fear falls through—
Fear falls through, and there isn't anything else on the horizon.
Young Republicans?
Young Republicans just fell through. That's bad. We were gonna have some fun. So right now I'm looking for a job in the computer field, with my friend David Kamm, who's a drummer for the Young Republicans. He hasn't called me back. He's given my résumé to the, to his boss, and I haven't heard back yet.

OPPOSITE— *Fear, from left: Andrew Jaimez, Scott Thunes, Lee Ving, and Sean Cruse.*

Chapter Sixteen

Compliment Me and I'll Kill You

Now, you've mentioned several . . . You've used the phrase "caustic, caustic personality." Um, you know, people calling you an asshole, all these sorts of things. Um . . . What would it take . . . What would it take to have . . . What am I trying to say here?

[Laughs.]

Okay. Isn't the pleasure or the release or whatever of playing in a good band, can't that make somebody strong enough to take anything, no matter how bad it is? Or does everyone have a breaking point?

Show me a good band. Name me a good band. Tell me what you think a good band consists of, and I'll tell you why—if I know that band and I know those people—I'll tell you why there is tension in that band. And music very rarely, for the people who perform it, releases tension. It almost always increases it. For any level. Whether you're performing for fun—you might have a problem performing in front of people. You perform with a person you're in a relationship with, which most of these coed bands have problems with, your relationship is going to carry over into the music. End of story. Ah, there's always a reason why music will not help you be a nice person. And it doesn't— You know, why should a good musician be a nice person? There's no connection. Tension is increasing, and we all have our own issues, and everybody's a human being. I don't understand why there is a, what a perfect band consists of.

Well, okay. Not in terms of a perfect band, but like . . . Okay, this CD here, this is my new favorite CD, Make a Jazz Noise Here. *And you're a young man, and I feel it would be sad if you never did anything this good again because you can't get in a band.*

It wouldn't be my fault. That band happened at that particular point of time because of the person who was in control of the funding and what the art that he preferred to convey to the world consisted of. Frank was a special case. He put up with a bunch of shit to allow the 1988 tour to work when it did. He loved having the horns, but I . . . If he could have gotten humanistic performances out of a Synclavier, he would've used that instead because what he wanted was all the juice with none of the blood. And that . . . All those albums have blood on every track. There is danger inherent in everything on *Make a Jazz Noise Here* and, uh, and, uh—

This—

[Raises hand.] *Don't* tell me! [Pause.] *The Best Band You Never Heard in Your Life.* Ahhh . . . Even the standardized performances, even if they were standardized every night, there was danger lurking behind every single note. You had no idea what was going to happen to the energy level or the tension because the tension was always there. My music I dig the tension in because of the modern classical music that I've heard; I know that it can coexist with normalcy. Frank is a big fan of that.

But! I don't need to do that ever again. I don't need to play in that kind of improvisatory glory again because it has been expressed perfectly in that arena.

But doesn't—

[Shouts.] WHY WOULD ANYBODY want to redo, relive this album?

Well, don't you get pleasure out of it? Don't you want to do it again?

I haven't listened to it in three years.

I-I can't understand that. I mean, it's such a brilliant album. You know—

[Shouts.] OH! OH! OKAY! You know a reason, right now, why I never listen to it? It's got fucking those *[sic]* asshole horn players all over it.

Okay.

It's got them everywhere. I listen to it, I see their faces. Now, when I listen to *Best Band You Never Heard,* it's *Frank's* music. They're Frank's *tunes.* Tunes that I grew up with, tunes that I think are *glorious.* I never, ever got to hear or play, ah . . . "Cruising for Burgers"? "Cruising for Burgers"? Um . . .

I think . . . I think that's right.

Yeeeeah. It's not on . . . [Claps hands.] "Cruising for Burgers"! I never knew that song. I never knew the glorious gloriousness of playing that solo. I love that solo section. And even on this album, he cuts off the last chord. My favorite part of the song is the payoff. And he cut it off and starts "Advance Romance" with the ugliest guitar noise in the universe. [Shouts.] AWRENG-RAYNG-RENG! I cannot *stand* listening to that. It's so absolutely painful. It's the exact wrong production decision to make. Hit the *chord! Then* go into "Advance Romance." But *don't* replace my favorite bit of music with my least favorite bit of music. And I loved playing "Advance Romance," but that was wrong. That was a really, really wrong decision.

Okay. Um . . . Saturday, you referred to yourself several times as a "musical has-been." So right now you're—

That was mean!

That was mean?

That was purely for journalistic format to do that. But that was good. I'm going to answer that.

Well, if you—

No! Don't-don't-don't-don't hedge! I'm going to—

No, I'm not hedging! I'm trying to talk! Jesus! Okay. Now you are a doorman at a club—

That's right.

—and you're looking to do computer programming?

Right. No! No. Computer anything. Computer anything.

Computer anything. Now again, I mean, I have to ask you because you're somebody with a gigantic talent, I mean . . . Can you see how some of us might see how that's a tragic waste?

No, because it's your fault.

It's my fault?

It's the audience's fault for being party to rock bullshit, for being able to accept the false truths that leaders of bands must, by definition, present to the world so that people think they're cool. If anybody on the face of the planet knew what Steve Vai and Dweezil Zappa were really like . . . I mean, Steve's had a career. Dweezil's never had a career. He might have at one point deserved it purely musically, but as a person, it is . . . He doesn't deserve anything. If you want to look at me and what I deserve, you letter writers, I don't deserve anything either because I'm a fucking asshole. But I'd rather be a fucking asshole who can express himself wherever and whenever I want to—and I have problems just in my regular lifestyle; it's not like it's just purely musical. I don't deserve what I got from Frank. I truly understand for myself that it was an absolute fluke of timing and nature that Frank wanted what I had to offer him at that particular point of time. Nothing else matters. I'm a good bass player, fine. I'm a great bass player, great. Think whatever you want. But I'm Scott Thunes first and foremost. Always have been. That's where most of those problems come from.

But! It is . . . I deserve the happiness that I can get from within my chosen lifestyle. Not musical glory. I do not deserve musical glory. Nobody does, unless they are golden. And I don't know anybody who's golden.

What about just the raw ability that . . . Someone with as radical an approach to the bass as [yours] would, I think, deserve to have people hear this.

Where? Where are you going to find a group of people that *I* could work with and express myself within the confines of happiness? All of this [points at my pile of CDs] that you have listened to and loved was born from almost virtual, total emotional degradation, and I'd rather not touch the damn thing again until I can be happy doing it. Which is why I'm doing demos for my friends. Which is why I'm gathering every night with as many of my friends as possible because I spent ten fucking years in Los Angeles trying . . . I didn't *even* try to become a musician because I was pretending that that was how you do your career. And I missed my friends, and I missed happiness, and I will do anything to keep ahold of it. I would much rather make eight dollars an hour working at the door of the Paradise Lounge than play *Make a Jazz Noise Here*–type music with a bunch of people, going out on the road, being away from my wife, and making the amount of money I would end up making.

I only got a good wage from this 1988 tour because Chad Wackerman said he could not work for anything less than twenty-five hundred dollars a week. And Frank was about to pay him thirteen hundred. We ended up with a compromise of two thousand dollars. So all the guys who'd been with the band before got two thousand. Everybody else in the band got thirteen hundred. Last time I went out with Steve Vai, I got 250 dollars—not a week, but just for this one gig. But before that, I got seven hundred a week, and twice I went out with him and got five hundred a week. Music doesn't pay. It's not worth it for me to leave my wife. And if I wasn't happy in my relationship, anything would be a reason to leave. And that's what most musicians do. They don't have a reason to stay at home because it means that they're not getting glory. They're not fucking chicks; they're not drinking themselves into a stupor every night; they're not finding cocaine in the pockets of crewmen. They're not getting the glory they feel they deserve, the level they deserve. My glory comes from the smile I get from my wife every day. I didn't get *shit* from any of these musicians except shit! While I was expressing my innermost desires through my musical expression and, and it was the only thing— Ah, I'm not going to say it was the only thing that was keeping me *alive*. I don't *know* what was keeping me alive. I had a job to do, I had to present myself to Frank every morning.

The music isn't worth it. Being in a band isn't worth it. Going out on the road isn't worth it. You would have to find a bunch of people to play with me and my friends that I have here. None of us . . . There aren't enough of my friends to form a band right now. And if we did, it would still be somebody else's music. So I'd still be going out and helping my friend Geoff's songs or my friend Jerry's songs or something like that.

The last band I was in, here in the Bay area, I broke up within two weeks. I broke up a band that had been together for two and a half years. At least that's one of the stories. The other story is that the two guys who were the main songwriters couldn't get along in the arena of actually writing songs, and a desperate change needed to be made. But the impetus to break up was me and my big mouth. And even then, I was putting myself out on a line to actually even play with these guys because they went on down to Los Angeles every once in a while. They'd leave for a weekend. I'm not gonna fucking leave my wife for a weekend! I don't mind playing in a band and playing music and, you know, having free beer and scoping chicks and playing pool and stuff like that, but I can do that around the corner. I can go with my wife to a bar, you know. It's much more fun than being in a band.

You're playing with your friends now. Aren't you worried that, if you do get a band together with your friends, the same thing will happen?

No, because I *won't* get in a band with my friends. Because I will only be helping them do what they want. And those, those things that die, the things in bands that die, were inherent in the bands themselves, not within me. I am a strong enough personality to-to show *other* assholes what kind of assholes they are, that they don't deserve to be together. Most bands don't deserve to be together. Most bands don't have good enough songs to convey to the world. They don't . . . People don't deserve to have

their music presented to the rest of the world. You are a lucky, motherfucking fucker to be able to stand up on stage and have somebody stare at you for five minutes. Ninety-eight percent of the people that are out there do not deserve it for a *second,* let alone having a career built on it.

Okay, but there are bass players that would kill to play on the number of albums you've played on.

Then kill! Go ahead and kill! [Laughs.]

There are going to be a lot of people that are going to think you're an idiot for throwing all this away.

I didn't throw *anything* away! *They* threw *me* away. I didn't leave Los Angeles until I couldn't get a gig for two years. There's no way I'm going to stay in Los Angeles for two, for-for . . . Okay, I *did* stay in Los Angeles for a second after I wasn't need-ed anymore. I stayed there for a couple years, but I was with a girlfriend; I was in love; I was having a good time. And when that ended, we decided to move up here. And so the plan was already in motion to get away from Los Angeles, even while I was still playing and working. Because I played with Frank for the first four tours; the first three tours, I was living in San Francisco. I'd go down for rehearsals and come back up here. There's no difference in the arena in which you do your, the physical arena in which you do your work. It's the mental arena, and my mental arena is nobody deserves anything. Your music, if you're lucky, make a tape of it. Mike Keneally spent years just mail ordering his cassettes. I don't think he made a dime off it. I can't imagine he made a dime off it, but his music was being disseminated through the universe. If people like it, they'll ask for it, great. He makes albums; some of them sell, some of them don't; it's no big deal.

But! You don't . . . You don't kill for a musical gig! It's not worth it. These musicians that are going to school and learning how to be musicians, you're not learning how to be a fucking rock star! You're not learning how to be famous! You're learning how to play music. That's *it!* You don't deserve to do anything with that. It doesn't mean that you get a band. It doesn't mean that you hook up with friends. It doesn't . . . mean . . . *dick.* You don't *deserve* anything. You spent five thousand dollars for school for a year? Great! You spent five thousand dollars on school; you now know that. Now get a job! And I don't mean in the musical world. I mean, get a *job.*

Okay, but I think it's possible that if somebody listens to the CD Does Humor Belong in Music? as a bass player and then listens to Make a Jazz Noise Here and listens to how there's, there's an amazing scope . . . It's almost like it's two completely different players. This may actually—listening to only these two CDs—may actually change somebody's approach to how to play music.

Good! It's cheaper than going to school.

Well, you're the guy who's doing these CDs, so wouldn't it be a shame if more and more young players didn't have the opportunity to hear what you have to offer?

They just did. Those two albums are out. They can buy them.

What else do they need to know? How many more albums of my performance do they need to hear before they get it?

As many as possible.

No.

More and more.

Then you're getting into the arena of how much do they need to know about me to make it knowledgeable. If they hear more albums, will they learn more? Or if they learn about what I think about what I played, will they learn more? Would they even understand it, even if I were able to tell it? Because really, all it is is music theory. I learned a little bit of music theory; I liked the melodies that I'm hearing in my head; I know what can go against a certain chord a certain way. I . . . What I learned at music school was that what modern music does is—you can play any note against any chord and make it mean something. You've only got twelve notes and you play a note that's exactly *one* half step higher than your tonic key, and you've already got a flat-nine chord. Flat nine is the most dissonant interval we have in Western music, and for thirty years it's been on every jazz album. You've heard it a thousand times. A flat-nine chord is, uh, a diminished seventh chord on the five-scale degree. Right? With the bass missing. Something like that.

I mean it's, all these . . . Every note you need is available to you, and you can use it. But if you don't know how you're using it or where it resolves, you're an idiot. You shouldn't be in music. That's all I'm doing. I learned a couple of simple laws, and I utilized them. If you can't get that from two or three improvisatory bass lines of mine, then you're not going to get it in two years of schooling. It's gonna be shoved down your throat, and you're *still* not going to get it.

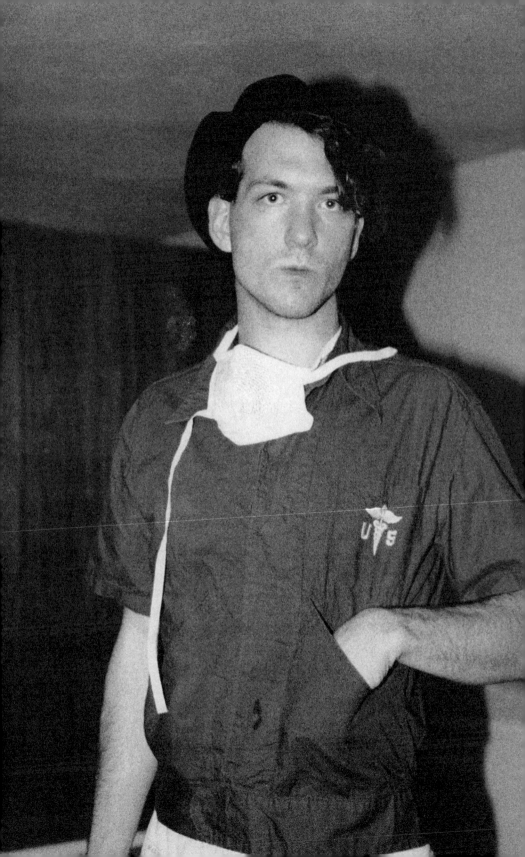

Chapter Seventeen
Antitechnique

So how does somebody develop a skill in improvising? How did you do it?

I was taught; I was given jazz lessons at a very early age, in my, very early part of my development. My mom got me a couple of bass teachers, and one of them was a guy named Marty Fuetsch, and he basically gave me jazz lessons. We learned how to listen to Ron Carter playing behind Sonny Rollins. I learned that these are the arenas in which you can maneuver tonally, and I utilized the concept of added tone chords to rock. Most of the time when I'm playing weird stuff against normal-sounding stuff, I'm adding a whole other chord. I'll be playing three actual notes, or I will be playing parts of these other chords against them. That's either polytonal or bitonal classical music or it's jazz because a lot of jazz chords are nothing but one chord superimposed over another, either a solo bass note or another chord. And it's the simplest thing in the world. I just give . . . I just gave away two thousand dollars' worth of lessons right now.

All you have to do is sit at a piano, play a chord down here, play a different chord up here, and you've got either classical music, modern classical music, or jazz, depending on how close the voicings are and what the spread is and what the difference in the two chords is. You've got every chord you'll ever need. You've got every bit of information at your fingertips, quote–unquote at your fingertips, right there, and there's nothing else I needed to know. Nobody sat around with me—since I was an adult—and said, "You know, your sound palette, your tonal palette is very limited." I'm a bass player. It *should* be limited. I should be doing way less. I shouldn't ever even *have* this knowledge! How many bass players, besides having the authority of the riff . . . The riff can take you into an amazing array of tonal arenas, but if you don't have the riff behind you to support your thought, what are you going to do? How are you going to live your life? Are you going to play a counter-melody? Are you going to invent a melody against something? You're gonna play a chord against something? A chordal pattern? An arpeggiated pattern against something? Or you're gonna play the tonic fucking note? You have very few choices: riff, melody, chords, arpeggiations. That's it.

So within these limited choices, then how is it you manage to improvise things that don't repeat themselves? I told you I listened to twenty CDs, and I didn't hear . . . I can hear lots and lots of bass players that fall in love with one riff that comes out in their improvisational lines and, you know, you don't seem to repeat yourself, and you get a melodic sense that is almost completely absent from 90 percent of other bass players out there. Is this what you were just talking about now?

No.

No?

No. On the one hand, I *have* repeated myself. Frank taught me a very good lesson one year. It was very painful, and it was very subtle, and it was painfully delicious. Aaah . . . Eighty-four tour, Ike Willis had given me a demo tape that most of the songs ended up on, the first album. I *guess* they're on the album, I don't know. Um . . . The demo tape kicked butt, and the album that he made from it is a bit weak, but there are several incredibly great songs on this demo tape, performed really well with really high energy, with very good friends. Really amazing, and I still have that tape floating around somewhere. And one of the songs has this bass line which is a very . . . It's The Riff. And it's very guitaristic, but it's funner than hell to play. And in 1984 I'd been listening to the tape a lot, and to make people in the band smile, you do certain things. You catch their eye; you do this thing, and you make fun. In this case, I used this bass line a lot because I enjoyed seeing, that year I enjoyed seeing Ike Willis happy and smiling and being goofy.

So I played this riff that he wrote underneath, oh, about a month's worth of Frank's solos. And Frank was in the middle of putting *Guitar* together, and he invited me over to the house one night; and I sat, and he said, "I put a bunch of solos together." And he had combined probably about eight or nine guitar solos on tape in a row that all had this riff underneath it. I'd just gotten bored; I wasn't supporting Frank in his solos, and he showed me up for the, for the lameness I had conveyed to him. He was paying me to be Scott Thunes, and I was . . . It was part of my buffoonery, but it was also part of my own agenda, and that,

that was, that was hurtful. But he was more hurt than I was, so, you know, he got the raw end of the stick.

That's one side of that—is I repeat myself in certain apparently humorous but actually nonhumorous arenas. And the other end of that is I have no idea what I'm going to play when I am doing this improvisatory universe. Because the whole point of playing with Frank is to react to what he's doing. And, uh, one of the things I like to hear is stacked fifths. Stacked fifths are very pretty; they're very open; you can stack several of them together, and you don't get too far outside of the tonal realm pitch. His favorite chord, Frank's favorite chord anyway, is the two chord, which is instead of C-E-G, it's C-D-G. And of course, if you transpose the D up an octave, you've got C-G-D. Two fifths. Now, you go to C-G-D-A-E-B, all you've got is a thirteen, nine, and a major seventh. Put them all together on a white-key chord, you've got six notes, and they're all pretty, especially if you stacked them in fifths. You've got your overtones working for you.

In the bass realm, it's so easy to make great music just using these bass notes because they can either be melodic or they can be the basis of a new chord. And that's a way to not repeat yourself that sounds, to *repeat* yourself that sounds like you're *not* repeating yourself. Because if you can get away with one-five, you can get away with five-nine because it . . . You're actually changing the key, but you're not. You're totally within the same key, and it's very frightening to attempt to explain this to somebody without sounding like, I don't know, an egomaniac or a teacher or something like that because, to me, it's obvious. It doesn't look like anything. It's stacked fifths on the piano, and it . . . They're just these notes. They're just these white keys. But when I play them with Frank, it opens up his music because nobody else is doing that. They stick with the riff; they stick with one note; they're afraid to play anything because any other note—it takes you away from the essence of the song. But if you're not in a song realm, you're improvising.

Now all of a sudden, this is where it gets hairy because why are you improvising? Are you improvising because there's a solo section in your song? Or are you improvising because you're playing jazz? If you're playing jazz, none of the notes matter. And if you're improvising in a rock work, you're leaving the riff, which most guitar players won't let their bass players do at all anyway. So bass players never learn autonomy, which is basically all that I did. I-I expressed my autonomy at all points in time, even during the songs. When I'm supposed to be playing certain riffs, I expressed my autonomy by "I'm going to decide to play the melody now." If I'm in a band, and some guy, the leader, turns around and says, "What the *fuck* are you doing?" I'll say, you know, "Tell me not to do it. Although now I don't want to be in this band anymore."

Because that's what I do. Most bass players don't ever get the chance because they don't learn autonomy. They don't have any interest in being autonomous. They have an interest in being in a rock band. They'll do anything to keep their gig. It is absolutely pointless to want to keep the gig just to keep the gig. You want to be yourself, and if you as a bass player are the guy or girl who wants to just be happy because they get to be on stage every night, then it doesn't matter what you play. And most rock bands are that exact same way. It doesn't matter what you play. If you got a new song, you should be happy to be playing that really cool bass line. Or if you're in a really great band with your pals, it doesn't matter what you play. That's why we've got so many jammin' seventies rock bands going on now because everybody's missing that. The tunes could still be good, and you could still have a good time, but what are you going to do as a bass player when you're rocking out in this improvisatory section in this rock band? You still have to keep [the] groove. And I never cared about the groove.

Why not?

It . . . I was not taught that it was something that was important. I listened to modern classical music, and the music I liked didn't have a groove. The rock music that I liked, when it was, when it was new wave or punk music or rock music, that bass player was doing what he wanted to do in that rock band. I never got a chance to be in that band. When I *was,* I was doing it pretty much ironically. Being in a rock band is a very strange thing. You either play songs that you love . . . You either are in a band with your pals . . . Being a bass player's even worse because very rarely are you writing the music. You're doing what your guitar player's telling you. So you are distanced from the music by however many levels you choose. I was always distanced from everything. I never wrote anything, and I was never asked to contribute. So it was always me being in this orchestra. And that forced me at gunpoint to be autonomous. I had no choice in the matter. I don't want to sit there and be the music robot. You can't. I *can't!* Even if I wanted to, I can't. And I've done rock albums, and I don't sound like anybody else because I'm either Scott Thunes being forced into this small hole, or I'm being Scott Thunes and that's fine.

I don't listen to my records and think they're amazing. I think they're derivative, and they sound like other people, and I'm not as good as *that* bass player and all that kind of crap; and so it doesn't matter what I think because, if I'm wrong, then I have no idea what I'm doing. And if I'm right, then everybody who thinks I'm great is full of shit.

[Several huge explosions, either backfires or shotgun blasts, are heard outside in the street. Thunes jumps and then smiles.]
WOWWWWW!

What was that?

I don't know! Beautiful! I *love* that!

[The tape recorder is turned off for a few minutes. We go to the window but can't see anything unusual. While we're up, we get beer for him and coffee for me, and he suddenly begins talking about Andy Prieboy. We sit down at the kitchen table again.]

Uh, yeah, so that's the single.

So Andy Prieboy . . .

Andy Prieboy was when . . . I . . . He was in a band called Eye

Protection in the early—in the late seventies, in San Francisco. And they weren't really a punk band, but they came about because of the rock insurgence, the punk rock insurgence, *re*surgence, and he actually had two horns. He would hire high school guys to come in and do horn parts because he actually was very orchestral-minded. He would do stuff like, uh [swings arm, conducting in deep, heroic tone of voice], "One-five! One-five! One-five! One-five!" at the ends of his songs and stuff. Very, very excellent dresser, uh, natty master of the universe, and very stylish. Very cool, calm, very . . . Tallest, thinnest guy in the universe, and his music was very quirky. It was classic San Francisco quirk rock. And he became the lead singer for Wall of Voodoo, and I'd go see them play every once in a while.

And I was sitting in my favorite haunt in Los Angeles, Double Rainbow Ice Cream, on Melrose, and he would come in all the time because he worked with some people at [a gift shop-bookstore-art gallery called] the Soap Plant, and he lived at the house of Billy what's-his-name [Billy Shire], the guy who owns the place. And he came in one day, and I said, "You are doing music? Why aren't you using me?" And he goes, "Oh, naah, I'm not really doing that much. I'm just kinda doing demos." And I said, "Well, I'd love to work with you. I'd work for free." And he goes, "For *free?* Okay!" And he sat me down, and he said, uh, "I've got work, but I can only pay seventy-five dollars." He thought I wouldn't work for seventy-five dollars a song. And since I wasn't working at all, I was very happy to make that seventy-five dollars a song, especially since he fucking worked so *much!* Every single night he was in [the] MCA [Publishing] demo studios [in Universal City], recording demos until four o'clock in the morning. And so I got-I got-I got four nights a week worth of work out of this guy. And all his demos ended up on the album, and it was really great. And he was really wonderful, and I've been trying to get on the road with him ever since.

But he doesn't have a record label that will give him a budget. So he goes out with his girlfriend, Rita [D'Albert, former guitarist of the Pandoras], and they do a duo. And so he hasn't had enough money for a bass player in all these years, and so no matter that I've been on both of his albums . . . The second album just came out and just immediately tanked because the record company died as soon as it came out. This brand-new album, which he spent three years on, dead in the water. And he's just the coolest guy, and I'd love to work with him, and that would be a really great operation because we've been through all our weird negativity and shit, and we know exactly what each other is about. That would be really fun. But he might hire a drummer who's a pinhead. And you know about that stuff.

   Sure. Well, okay . . . Um—
   Where were we?

Chapter Eighteen
And Don't Call Me a Bass Player

Okay, we were talking about, right before the shotgun blasts . . . Okay. Let me, let me . . . I'll come back to it. I just wanted to ask you: I was told by Mike Keneally that you might not appreciate being called a bass player, and you sort of touched on this yourself. Can you explain that again? What's the problem with being called a bass player?

Got it. [Sighs.] When I learned how to play the bass, it was by default. I didn't really choose it for myself. My mother brought one home one day. I was too young to appreciate any musicality about it whatsoever, so within six months, I stopped. When I started up again, it was because I saw that my brother and his friends were having so much fun, and it was an instrument I had picked up already. I'd had it underneath my fingers. So by the time that my friend Joe and I were playing bass at each other and being the Dynamic Duo, I had gotten the mechanics underneath my hands, and they were doing Doors and Cream and some other kinds of blues tunes. That's where I stopped appreciating the blues, after I'd played it for the first three years of my musical experience. It was a good basis for improvisation, and I had a couple of good bands who were well versed in it as extensions to whatever the blues universe had to offer. The blues didn't offer anything to me harmonically after that. People understand—*don't* understand—why I don't like the blues, and it's very difficult to explain.

But! As a bass player, it's very easy to love the blues because it's so easy: Every song is the same. Oh, there's *so much* difference, I know, it's so sad. Aah . . . But playing the bass was a way to get into music. It was a way for my musicality to be expressed. I didn't even know I had the musicality, I was just able. And within a short amount of time, I exhibited talent for this specific instrument. When I went to [the] College of Marin, I played in the jazz band, concert band, the night concert band for all the adults, the retired professionals, uh, orchestra, and chamber music. I was also in chamber singers and the choral group and was doing every musical thing I could possibly get my hands on, including performing some simple piano pieces. And the bass helped me as a young person to be equal to the adults that were going to college. They weren't eighteen-year-olds. This was a community college. There were a bunch of adults there, real adults, forty or fifty years old. And [drummer] Terry Bozzio had just finished going there when I started going there. And he was the famous son of the Bay area. You know, he'd gone to the College of Marin and had gone on to great glory. And I was The Chosen next, and I would kick butt in any of my musical adventures, and I had a great year.

The bass was the only thing I had at that time. I had the bass. I was in the band. I was playing jazz. I was very good. I was learning tons of stuff in a very short amount of time. I was soaking up information from all sources. And I never . . . I don't think of a time when I thought of myself as a bass player. I just was *the* bass player. I was the bass player in that band. I was the bass player in the jazz band. I was a *musician.* I was striving to be a musician. I wanted to be a musician. I had already experienced an epiphany by seeing this piano player, Art Lande, playing, where I said to myself, "I will never be a musician." If I'm not a musician, am I a bass player? Aren't bass players musicians? It's all semantics. I was a big fan of words since day one, and I just choose not to accept the mantle because I've never seen Flea

play, but I've heard him on records, and I've seen his videos, and he does something that I cannot do. And when I put myself out as a bass teacher, I've gotten a couple of students, and I tell them immediately, "I don't slap. I don't know how. I couldn't *begin* to guess what the mechanics are of that." I have a friend, Mark Burlingame, who is an okay bass player. He can slap like a maniac. He's not even in a band. He's in chemistry. He's getting his Ph.D. in chemistry.

Being a bass player means caring about the bass, and that means the *function* of the bass as well. The function of the bass is very important to a rock band, and I've never, *ever* been able to, without irony, perform that function. I think it's not my purpose in life, and that's what a bass player does. He either fulfills the need with emotion and depth for the purpose of being in that band, and I've never had that. I've always been able to play the bass well enough to be able to work at a couple of gigs. But those gigs fell into my lap. Very, very Zen, very Tao situation, where I go about music waiting for the next thing to fall into my lap. Because I don't know how to search for anything, which is one of the reasons I left Los Angeles in the first place: because I don't know how to hump my, my act on my shoulder and lug it from agent to agent. The company wants to pick me up, fine. If I can't get any more gigs, fine.

But! The actual role of the bass player does not interest me, has never interested me, and I don't understand how it could interest anybody else. Because it's not a glory position. It's the ultimate nonglory position. Singers, guitar players, drummers, bass. That's how it goes, in order of importance.

Okay, you had your epiphany. I can tell you for a fact . . . I know this, that people will listen to this CD or other things you've done and say to themselves, "I'm not a bass player," after listening to you play. They will do that.

Well, I hate to call them fools, but they don't know anything about music. Why does it . . . What does it matter if you're a bass player? Pick another instrument that you can express yourself on. I express myself on the bass because I've been playing it for twenty-five fucking years, and its-its visualization of the key-board is simple to me. It's simpler than the guitar, which has that fucking third between the G and the B and throws off my whole frame of reference. And the joy of playing the bass is the joy of having my voice come out in an instrument. And I don't understand how that makes me a bass player. Semantically, I cannot understand how that makes me a chosen role model because it's the voice that's important, not the instrument. Everybody else is trying to make the bass the voice. Stu Hamm playing the [Ludwig van Beethoven] *Moonlight Sonata*? It's an ugly sound. Don't do it! Step *away* from the bass. If you think the sound of the bass is more important than your own personal voice, then you've missed the point of music completely. I would much rather not play the bass ever again, for the rest of my days, so that I can have my voice. And I am able to speak my piece with my friends and my professional cohorts, to a certain degree; that is satisfactory to me. Much more than in the bass arena because I am constantly thwarted.

Frank was one of the only people that didn't thwart me. As soon as I started playing with Dweezil, who was my next musi-cal group after Frank, I was starting to get pressurized to per-form the bass function. When I was in the first couple of years of actually being in the Dweezil rock band, which was from '88 to '92, whenever it was, the first couple of months of that were Josh, Dweezil, and I in a room playing Dweezil's music. But what we did was we worked on the music. We played the tunes which were good riffs, we orchestrated so that there was depth and interest, and I was . . . My voice was necessary to add to the texture, to fulfill a certain countermelodic need that the riffs required, and I was able to tell Josh exactly, specifically what kind of drum patterns to play that would mesh well with the rest of what we were doing. That's what I did.

My voice was heard verbally and musically, and then when that stopped because we added in a second guitar player who filled up my areas with his voice, I became a bass player. My verbal voice and my musical voice were no longer necessary. I remained in the band for fear of rejection outside of that small musical sphere, and I wasn't getting it at home. So I needed some kind of expression. After that, everything else since then has been very limited. The worst kind of limited for my personal voice.

Okay. Although I understand what you're saying, is . . . Okay, you said you can't really stand as a role model for a lot of different reasons, the bands you played with, you said it was a fluke.

But! Okay, talking strictly from a musical point of view, what you're doing on the bass has the same impact as say, Stu Hamm doing his **Moonlight Sonata** *to people who say, "Whoa! It opens up new possibilities." What you're doing is you're taking . . . Your playing has just as much impact without all the sizzle, without all the tapping, the slapping, all this sort of stuff. And that's very unusual for somebody simply with a pick and his fingers playing riffs. So you* **can** *serve as a role model because people will—their world will be opened up. For bass players, this is an approach they've never thought of, somehow.*

That's got to be impossible because I was not the first and only person to do this. I had to have gotten it from somebody else. How come they don't listen to that person as well?

Who'd you get it from?

[Led Zeppelin's] John Paul Jones.

Yeah?

Yeah! He was my role model in the meshing of riffing with his own personal melodic voice. And he actually played . . . When he wasn't playing the riffs, when he was given a moment, he played melodies. And I know for a fact he's not the best bass player in the world, but neither am I, and that was not his purpose. He was not supposed to be a great bass player. Most guitar players don't want a *great* bass player to play off against because they're going to be as good as them, and most people don't want the-the complicated dynamic interplay. They more prefer an orchestrated interplay. And that's what I performed: an orchestrational interplay with any other instrument. I don't think of the guitar as my foil. It just happens in rock bands that he's the only, he or she is the only person there who's actually doing something. Most of the time their stuff is fairly rigid, and so it gives me tons of room to be fluid against. And it's unfair that I should be given all this, uh-uh-uh, even *slight* attention for something that I don't feel pushed the boundaries of the instrument.

Not at all?

I don't see how.

So do you actually—

I haven't done anything that nobody else has done before. If I play a chord on the bass, all I'm doing is playing a fucking chord on the bass. I'm doing something absolutely wrong. I'm doing something that nobody would ever allow me to do. "Why are you playing a fucking chord on the bass?" Okay, you play a chord on the bass, it's either going to be a fake guitar voicing, which you can do for orchestration purposes . . . That's orchestration. That's . . . That has nothing to do with the bass. If I'm an arranger and my instrument of choice is the bass, then I have a requirement to enliven the proceedings melodically, if I have something to say in the melodic realm. Which most people do not. I don't think *I* do.

I don't think the things that I'm actually saying—standing alone—are important. It's the interplay with what else is going on. Nobody has thought of that. Nobody has been in the position to make that melodic chunk happen at that particular point in time. I happened to be there, I happened to find it. You know, geniuses say that it comes from somewhere else. All that is, I *know* what I'm doing. I don't, I don't think of it at the time I'm doing it, but the most important thing is that the sound has been made and created that has not been made before. But that's not a bass-playing thing. It just happens to be on the bass that that thing is, is being created. [Pause.] Um . . . I forgot the question.

Oh, ah . . . Okay. I was just going to ask, do you repudiate completely the idea that your playing is of any value to, to young people who might look to you as a role model?

No. Yes. [Laughs.]

No, yes?

Yes. I do not repudiate the idea that it has any value but not as a role model. Because the value is only that-that something is being done that *can* be done. You don't have to be a bass player all the time if you don't want to. I had no choice because I can't be a bass player. I don't *want* to be a bass player; I have no *interest* in being a bass player; I don't want to fulfill that role. I want to be Scott Thunes, who has that voice. And even in Fear, which you think punk music is very simple . . . Retard! Don't even talk to me about punk music if you think it's simple. It's not supposed to be simple; it *never* was. Ahh . . .

Anyway, whatever you think punk music is, Fear has always had odd meters. He started off in jazz, Lee did, and his music has odd meters, weird arrangements, mathematical, geometric progressions. If you just look on the fingerboard, he's moving in, in major third down, tritone up, major third down, tritone up, which if you look on the keyboard is one string down, one fret up, next string back up, one fret up. It's very mathematical, something very simple, but harmonically you go, "Oh my God, how did he think of that?" Just look at the keyboard thing. "I'm not going to play this blues riff. I don't have to play a blues riff. Everybody else does because they don't even, they can't even imagine what goes on outside of the box." *Everything* happens outside of the box. Everything. Everything musical happens outside of the box. If you know guitar, bass, you know what I'm talking about.

The music has always been *my* role model. If there isn't anything juicy in it, I don't have anything to play against. And if I don't . . . Even if it is just simple chords and I'm given my arena, then it's still the song that I'm playing with, not myself. Ninety-eight percent of the time I'm not masturbating, I am actually attempting to have sex with the song. It's not me *against* the other instruments, which is what most guitar players would think if they heard what I did. It's too much. It's over the top. It's melodic. It's counterproductive.

I don't have an interest in being your foil. Most guitar players would rather do the bass parts themselves. If they had their druthers, if they were two people . . . "God, I wish that guy played more of what I want him to play."

You know, a lot of rock bands are good because they have different voices. That's what John Paul Jones did. His voice was heard in conjunction with what else was going on in all the other voices. And that shouldn't have worked at all because Jimmy Page, who is one of my favorite guitar players in the universe, is not a very good guitar player. But he's got great ideas, and he attempts to perform them. As a matter of fact, I'd say Jimmy Page was more of a role model for me as a bass player than anything else because he and I share, aah, uncouth tone. And I prefer the sound of the uncouth tone to the perfect and clean and produced and all that kind of stuff. And 98 percent of the time, somebody's going to want to produce my voice away. And I'm not interested in performing in an ensemble that doesn't have a use for my voice.

Chapter Nineteen

A Series of
Idiotic Questions

Is that why you went with a pick and the Fender Precision basses and things like that?

Um—

To get that specific voice and uncouth tone?

Yes. I heard Tom Fowler in Frank's album *Roxy and Elsewhere,* and he played with a pick and had a black P-Bass with a white pick guard. And that sound intrigued me. It growled. It was ugly. Yet he could play all these complicated riffs. And it didn't sound overly technical the way he did it. It sounded-sounded *cool.* It sounded really fuckin' cool. And it took me thirteen years to get a P-Bass. And in the first couple of years of playing with Frank, I played these Carvin instruments. That wasn't my voice. Also I was playing predetermined riffs on all these songs. Nineteen eighty-four was the first year I used the P-Bass in actuality. And he let me do anything I wanted, and what I heard of what I did that wasn't rancid was good. And in '88, when he gave me complete and utter carte blanche, I shone in the ultimate way that a bass player can shine. I had the tone that I wanted; I had the amplification that I wanted; I had the performer's arena. He lent me a wireless, and I jumped around; I rolled around. I always rolled around anyway, but this time with my bass. I laid on my back. I had an absolute wonderful time. Everything came together except happiness. I wasn't happy. The music was great; being with Frank was great, but everything else sucked. And the instrument itself begat my musical happiness because I had it all together, from . . .

You know, thinking as just a kid wanting to emulate his heroes, then I was the new Tom Fowler. And I was riffing, and I was sounding cool, and I was getting the growl in there, and I think Frank appreciated that growl. I think he had tired of perfection, and it was very dangerous to play with me. Because he had no idea what I was going to do, and he liked that because it made him play other things. But nobody really tried to give him a new tonal arena to play in. And the simplest expression of that is, if you're in the key of C major and I play in A-flat, that's . . . And I don't mean a high A-flat; I mean the lowest A-flat, a bass note below the chord, so that creates a new chord. In this case, it creates a C-augmented major seventh chord, ah, A-flat–augmented major seventh chord. And that's a really juicy chord, and it's really fun to play against because it's completely wrong. But all's you have to do is go to C major. All's you have to do is play in C major, and I'll make you weird.

And that's what I did in Frank, all the time. I gave him arenas that he himself knew existed in classical music and he knew could exist if he were able to turn around microsecond by microsecond and yell out, "B-flat! A-natural!" I did all that shit on purpose to freak him out and to give him joy, and his joy begat more joy within me and made me play weirder and weirder. So by the time '88 came around, and I'm doing eighth-note runs starting up at the top of the scale in the simplest song—[sings] *"Doo-doo-doo-doo, doo-doo-doo-doo, doo-doo-doo-doo, doo-doo-doo-doo"*—and he doesn't turn around except to smile at me, then, then my voice has been heard, and the song has been made different, which is what he liked to do anyway. He never had to do any orchestration in the bass because I would do that for him. And everybody else pretty much did what he told them to do, and he could rely on that, but he never knew what was going to come out of me. It was great.

Well, okay. You said that you had problems with drummers. It seems like you had almost this telepathy with some of the drummers, especially Wackerman. I thought you and he played really well. There's this echoing of rolls, drum rolls that you're echoing on the bass on the video for Does Humor Belong in Music? It seems to the uninitiated, who don't know the inside story, that you two were breathing together.

That's the stupidest thing I've ever heard.

Why?

Because I'm *listening* to him. That's all you're hearing. You're hearing me react to him. As a matter of fact, I'm being led around by the nose. If he knows for a fact that I'm the imitation maniac, he can utilize that at any time. I don't believe he did, but all I'm doing is saying to myself [sighs], "Oh, what else is there to react to? Listen to Frank; listen to the drums; listen to the keyboards. I know all the riffs that are in the song. At what point in time do I want to echo them? The only strange thing might be . . . *the drums!*" Maybe that's an orchestration that you're actually hearing that we decided on months in advance. There were a bunch of things like that that we would echo just for fun, not necessarily to keep from being bored but because the music allowed it, Frank allowed it, and we could do it; we thought of it, and it was good. And it sounded good, and it wasn't antimusical, and we continued to do it.

But! But if you want to think of the true essence of a moment that you're explaining, that maybe I am actually doing something, you wouldn't be able to get me to agree that Chad ever copied a riff that I did.

Really?

Yes.

Never?

I don't think he . . . As a matter of fact, I know for a fact that he turned me out of his monitors in 1988. He told the sound guy to have me completely out of his monitors, which is why in 98 percent of our downbeats, we're wrong.

Well, it just goes to show that if you don't know the inside story, then a lot of times you don't know exactly what is going on musically because—

[The first 120-minute cassette tape is full. I put in a new tape as Scott talks. I have to ask him to repeat what he said about the other band members while the recorder was down.]

Okay. Ninety-eight percent of the time they're shooting daggers at you . . .

Yeah, from behind. I can feel them. I know exactly what's going on, and I'm attempting to create music through the distressing surroundings that I find myself in.

Okay, so let me take a Pollyanna look. Uh, as bad as the circumstances were, you created great music. What could've happened if everybody loved each other and everything was going great? Would you have . . . Would the music have been taken to a much higher level?

Yes. We would have found ourselves, uh, happily intercommunicating instead of . . . One of the very first things that Frank does when you joined his band is he sits you down and he says, "This is how we work. I don't want you *copying* my riffs. I want you *supporting* them. I want you playing complementary motifs."

That's what he said to you?

Yes. To all of us. He gave us all *Shut Up 'n Play Yer Guitar* to show us how to improvise with him. Which is very strange because the whole concept of "Watermelon in Easter Hay"— Ever heard of the song?

Yeah.

You know what it means?

No.

Okay. You know what Easter hay is?

Easter hay? No. What?

Okay. Neither did I, but we all have seen it. In Easter baskets, you've got the green plastic furry stuff? He says that getting a good solo backing out of his musicians—this must have been in '77 or '76 or something like that because the song came out in 1980—getting a good musical backing out of his band was like trying to grow a watermelon in Easter hay. And this song, "Watermelon in Easter Hay," is nothing but a giant improvisation. You know, it's a riff, and he plays against it. But it's the simplest of riffs; it's a keyboard riff that everybody plays, that nobody is allowed to deviate from. I deviated a *lot.*

Against his will?

Oh, well, he never turned around and said, "Stop!" It's the Scott Thunes effect, baby.

And is this the sort of thing that led people to say you're abrasive and hard to get along with, because you don't want to compromise on stage?

No. It's definitely in my personal life. On stage stuff is, was only, was only turned into a negative by the people who didn't like that form of communication to begin with. Didn't want people to step outside their predetermined roles. They didn't realize, they honestly didn't realize the unspoken bond that Frank and I had in the string arena. *He* never told me what to do; *you* don't have the right to tell me what to do. Leave me alone. If I tell you to leave me alone, I'm abrasive. If you tell me what to do, I will get angry. If you continue to tell me what to do, I will get *really* angry. If you say something stupid, I will get angry. If you attempt to drag my conversation down to a moronic level, I will get angry; I will stomp out of the room; I will leave. I don't need your friendship. I don't need your low level of happiness. I need to hear beauty in verbiage and musicality. I mean, that's my requirement. And nobody else has that requirement. They need comfort; they need familiarity. [Pause.] I don't know where that went.

Well, okay, it went fine. It went fine. You said, though, that during this period you were having a lot of problems; you were desperately unhappy in your personal life. What

do you say to the person who says, "You brought it all on yourself. Mellow out! Go with the flow!" You know, all those kinds of things.

Yeah. Okay. I think what I wanted to go with the last question was . . . You wanted to know where, if we were all communicating together, if it would have gone to new levels.

Right.

Ahh . . . "Watermelon in Easter Hay" effect is that it happens when you least expect it. It happens no matter what else is going on in your life, and if you have something concrete to focus on, you're not going to end up in the musical universe. You're just going to be playing the riffs. And to lose yourself is to feel comfortable, is to have it all presented to you on a silver platter. That this is, that this universe has been built for your happiness. And I am, I am easily happy to just have an arena where my voice can be heard. If I have a drummer who is not playing with me or is playing against me, or their agenda is more important than the larger good, then there isn't anything for me to do except pull back, which is what I did quite a lot. I-I overstated my sadness; I wore my heart on my sleeve quite a lot, and for many months of that '88 tour I stood there like a robot. And fans would come up to me and say, "You looked like you were having a root canal." And I'd say, "You have no fucking *idea!*"

Especially since it didn't matter in the long run to the audience whether I was playing my ass off and fulfilling my "genius musical destiny" or being miserable and playing just the bass lines. It didn't matter. When I wanted to do it, it was okay, but if I didn't want to do it, it wasn't okay. They began to expect . . . I actually realized that they expected me to be performing, and if I am noticing that out of three thousand people in the audience, and every single one of them has their eye on Frank, no matter what else is going on on stage, I'm not performing. There's nothing to perform to. All I need to do is play the riffs that I'm getting paid to play. And that's the exact opposite from this exalted musical state that I guess the players in Miles

Davis's band got to every single moment of every single night because it must have been an absolute joy to play with Miles. He was probably one of the nicest people on the face of the planet. You catch my irony?

It's very important to realize that you are not listening to *musicians.* You're listening to *people.* And either those people are very happy to make the money and will go all out no matter what it is, no matter if there are six people in the audience, or you're dealing with a person who is used to a better form of expression and will not stand for it. I ended up being paid to stand on stage and make low-frequency noises at Frank's music a lot of the time in 1988. The stuff you're hearing on the albums that you like, *Make a Jazz Noise [Here]* and *[The] Best Band You Never Heard [in Your Life],* are the moments of emotional battle won with oneself. I don't care if I'm not going to be listened to: I'm going to do this for myself, and I'm going to do it for Frank. If I can get past my pain, I will actually do some playing. And I don't know if any of those epiphanies actually made it onto records. I don't know if there are some genius moments. If the genius moments are purely me just picking that one strange note and digging the sound, is that genius or is that twelve-note boredom? I've got twelve notes to play with. I'll pick *this* one! See what happens.

Well, okay. You seem to be implying that, a lot of what you did, your heart wasn't in it. And I would just say to you, if your heart was ever in it, nobody could touch you.

Right. Fine. Thank you.

Well, no, what I mean is: How are we going to get your heart back into it?

Why do you . . . Why do you *care?* I had that then because I was twenty-four. I'm not twenty-four any more.

Yeah, but I mean, presumably, as you continue growing, so will your music. You'll be playing different music at thirty-six than you did when you were twenty-four, so what I'm wondering is: What are you capable of now? If you win the

thirty-million-dollar lottery tomorrow, let's say, what would you do musically?

[Smiles tightly.] Mmmmmm.

Presumably you'd still be interested in music, wouldn't you?

Oh, absolutely. But not the bass. I would . . . I would orchestrate. Yup. I would write pieces that I would make other people play. And I would sit back, and I would watch.

And you would hire a bass player?

There would be no bass player in my music. If I had my druthers, I would never, ever write for a rock band. I have no interest in composing songs. Twice on the '88 tour I asked Mike Keneally and I asked Bruce Fowler to write me a piece of music. Ahh . . . Both of them are in their way geniuses and had a lot of musical talent and do a lot of strange things with your standard rock band orchestration. That's all it is. It's just an electric quintet. And I asked Bruce Fowler, I said, "I'll give you 250 dollars if you write me a ten-minute work using nine instruments." Which is the . . . Nine instruments is the orchestra used by Webern in the Concerto Opus 24. And [Bruce's] brother Walt said, "Two hundred fifty dollars? That's working awful cheap!" As if I wanted to keep the piece of music or only have the rights for it. I . . . It was a bribe, to get him to stop playing cribbage for a night. He could have done it in a night! He's never done it, as far as I could tell. I've heard his albums, and they're all for a rock band. Mike Keneally hasn't done it. He wanted me to write a string quartet arrangement to his piece *Airport,* which I wrote three or four bars of and then lost and couldn't get the inspiration back to finish it. And I was also angry about the Dweezil debacle. So I never got it together again.

But! The rock band is my least favorite ensemble for performing musicality. I . . . If I needed to have my music performed right now and the rock band was the only musical amalgam I could put together, I wouldn't know who to fucking hire. I wouldn't know who could play my music. I wrote out . . . [Composer Paul] Hindemith wrote a piano piece called *Ludus Tonalis,* which lasts about an hour. It's twenty-four fugues and twenty-four interludes, and I wrote out several of my favorite movements for two guitars and bass because most of them are three voices. I could have played all three of them if I were three people. But I could never, ever, to this day—it's been thirteen years—[have] been able to find musicians who could read music who played guitar and bass, who would want to sit around with me and play Hindemith's *Ludus Tonalis* orchestrated for three pieces. If I can't even get a rock band to do classical music, how am I going to get a rock band to do rock music? [Laughs loudly.] I love that! And that's much more important to me than the song because I can't really write songs. And if I do write a song, then it's on four-track, and I've played all the parts, and I don't need anybody to play it. And nobody's going to hear it except for my friends anyway. So . . .

Chapter Twenty

Songs and Pieces of the Heart

You can't write a song, but you can write music.

Right.

What's the difference?

The difference is that, when I sit down with a piece of paper—and I've only done this twice in the past fifteen years; it's not like I'm a composer at all, don't get me wrong—I thought of a reason why I wanted these two instruments to go together, the violin and cello. And I started writing down as much music as I could get out of four open strings. I mean, it can't be that hard. To make it *musical,* sure. I don't even know if I failed. I like what I wrote, and it worked out fine. And then I wanted to write another little section. So I'm sitting down, and I'm writing down ideas. And the ideas are lasting about forty-five seconds apiece. If I were to do that with a rock band, I would have to orchestrate the drums; I would have to orchestrate the guitar; I would have to orchestrate the bass; I would have to orchestrate a melodic instrument. If I'm writing for two instruments, I am writing notes down and having fun. If I were to orchestrate something for a rock band, I would have to work. It would have to be work, and there'd have to be a point. There'd have to be a reason.

Writing music is different from writing something for your chosen ensemble. Because I'm not in a band. I don't have to write tunes for my band. Most people have to write tunes for their band. They have to sit around with a guitar and think of a melodic and structural concept that, that hasn't been done before, that they can actually perform on their hands, and that they enjoy doing. That doesn't sound like much fun to me. I'd much rather write something that I think a couple instrumentalists will enjoy playing. I could write some guitar music if I wanted to, but *fuck* the guitar! Especially for any kind of classical thing. You know, it doesn't sound good when you play two or three weird-sounding notes together on a— Okay, it does. It sounds good on a guitar. There's a million ways to make it sound good.

But! But there aren't any people with rock sensibilities writing classical music. They're all classical musicians. They're all academicians. Fuck that noise! I am Scott Thunes writing music. If I were to sit down and attempt to write a song, I would have to do what I explained to you before: sit down and do something that hasn't been done before, something that my hands can perform, and something that is interesting to me. And that whole process sounds like work, and I'm not going to get anything out of it anyway except a bunch of music that I won't be able to get a bunch of other people to play. And if I do get them to play it, what does that mean? Does that mean I'm going to have to go out on the road? The whole prospect frightens the hell out of me. What the hell is the point? There aren't enough rock bands? I would much rather get paid a shitload of money, go out for a couple of months . . . I'd do, I'd do shitty music right now because I need the money.

You would *do it, or you* do *do it?*

I haven't done it, and nobody has offered.

But you would do it.

I would do it right now because I'm desperate. I've got tax problems up the yin-yang, and-and it gets ugly. It's something I can do; it's something I can make a quick amount of money at. But the only people who would hire me are these people who do complicated music that nobody likes, that they can't even afford to hire me.

In 1982, I sent a letter to the Gang of Four because I knew that they had lost their bass player. I said, "I'm available." I never heard from them. Uh . . . They Might Be Giants recently did a rock album with a live band, and I said to myself, "This bass player isn't really that good. He probably is just a local friend of theirs." I said, "I'm available." I wrote them a letter explaining—it was a three-page letter—explaining all the cool stuff that I found in their album. I found a quote from [Gustav] Mahler's Fifth Symphony in their album. I said, "Could you please, you know, make sure that the guys read this? But I also want to be put on the 'Hello CD' mailing list and on your fan club mailing list." So I got the "Hello CD" application and the fan letter, and that was it.

If I'm gonna go around and asking *[sic]*, and ask people if I can be in their band and not even get letters back, what's going to happen when I actually, really, really desperately want to do something? You work for it; you call them up all the time, okay. That happens. But-but I'm already a known quantity. They've heard my work—or they can if they wanted to—and they've heard the stories. If the stories are scaring them away, fuck them all!

Anyway, I don't want to deal with them because nobody is interested in what's going on with me. Nobody wants my voice in their music desperately enough to call me up and ask me to do it. The people, the gigs that I'm getting are from people who don't know shit about me. And then when they work with me, they never work with me again.

I did this album with Wayne Kramer, the guy from MC5. I went down there and I auditioned, and he had six more songs to do. He'd done the bass on six songs, and he had six more songs to do. I went down and I auditioned, and after I played, he drove me to the drop-off point and said, "Well, um, I'm gonna do the rest of the album myself. But I'm gonna be doing a bunch of music, you know, going out on the road again, starting in January." About two months later. "I'm gonna have about a year's worth of work." I said, "Cool." I went home. He thought about it, called me back. I'd already gone down to, gone back up north, and he said, "Actually, I'm wrong. I *would* like you to play on my album." So I had to fly back the very next day, and I went and I played six songs in two days, three songs a day. That was the last I heard from him. I read an interview in *CMJ* magazine where he said, "Oh man, yeah, I've had problems with bass players, man. The bass player that I was going to use, uh, couldn't get his passport renewed. We were going to Europe, Japan. He couldn't get his passport renewed because of the governmental shutdown, so I had to scramble to find a bass player that knew the material."

[Misunderstanding.] *So he called you back because he couldn't get . . . The next day . . .*

No, no! I went down and recorded the songs. Then I went home.

So are you the guy who supposedly couldn't get his passport renewed?

No! No! I never heard from him after I did the album and got my six hundred dollars.

So what was he blathering about?

I have no idea, but that's music in Los Angeles. And you can fucking have it.

Okay. You've told me so many stories now. You approached MIT [the Musicians Institute of Technology], BIT [the Bass Institute of Technology], uh—

Well, it's all . . . It's all one thing. I called them up and said I would like to be a bass teacher, and they said, "No thanks, we've already got Jeff Berlin." So I went down there a couple of months later and put flyers all around, and I didn't get one phone call.

Right. Why the hell is this happening?

Aaaahhhhh . . .

I mean, are you star-crossed?

Aaaahhhhh . . . I'm not star-crossed. I got to play with Frank Zappa for seven years. Fuck the rest of the music, man. I don't . . . I don't need it. I got to play with Frank, and even *that* was a pain in the ass.

But that's enough for you? That's really enough for you?
No! I wanna play other things! I wanna involve myself in
music in my own personal voice. I . . . During the '88 rehearsals,
when I was Clonemeister, Frank had me come up to the house
and listen to a bunch of music. And it was about four o'clock in
the morning, and we were finished. I said, "Frank? Whither
music?" He said, "I don't understand." I said, "You know, whither music? What about music?" He said, "You're gonna have to
explain yourself." I gave him a fifteen-minute question about
what was the purpose of being a musician in today's society. He
had just finished going to the American Society of Academic
Composers, and his valedictorian speech, or whatever you call
it when an emeritus, genius comes and talks to you . . . He says,
"All of you: real estate. None of you should attempt to write
music. We don't need you. Music doesn't need you."

So I'm asking him, "What's, what's the point? If you're playing good music, nobody understands it anyway. If you're playing bad music, they love it to death. I'm a guy who's been
playing with you, and this is good and that's bad . . . " And he
said, "Well . . . " He gave me a three-hour answer. He kept me
there until six or seven in the morning. And part of the thing
he said was "I think of all the people I know, you should be
writing classical music because you—" and not because I'm a
genius, not because I'm a musical wonderment, but because
"—I think you have a romantic vision of what it means to be
a classical composer."

He liked to say that I didn't know anything about the blues
and that Ike Willis didn't know anything about classical music,
and if we could mix our problems together, we'd be better musicians for it. He said that I had a romantic vision of what it meant
to be a classical composer and that I should write pieces so that
I could get burned, so that I could know what it's like.

So in 1991, I don't know where the inspiration came from,
but I ended up with six and a half minutes' worth of music for
violin and cello. I wrote it down; I put it in my computer; I
printed it out; I took it with me everywhere. I had that music

with me for about three years. And I printed it up, copied it, and gave it to six duos, all of whom said, "We desperately need material. We really want to work with this." I gave it to my brother-in-law in Germany, who works for a small opera company. He's got an entire orchestra of people to deal with. It's been four years. I haven't heard hide nor hair from him about that piece of music. I've given it to five or six people, and not one of them has sent me a rehearsal tape. Not one of them has called me or written me and asked me any questions. I've gotten not one performance out of it.

Friend of mine wrote a bunch of string quartets, and I went down to Menlo Park to help him record them. Not really produce but just, you know, he doesn't know anything about classical music, and he printed this stuff up on his computer. And I went down there, and I made sure that everything worked, as well as I possibly could. And the string quartet that performed was, was *lacking,* distinctly lacking. But at the very end, they decided to read through my string drill. I [had] brought the music with me. And of course, you know, it's too hard to sight-read. You have to sit with it for X amount of rehearsals, and then we fine-tune. But I'm sitting there, and I've got it on videotape of them performing my duo. It's really delicious. It actually sounds very good. I'm very pleased.

But! I can't get any of the really juicy stuff because this cellist is trying to read sixteenth-note C-flats in riffs and stuff like that, and it's not gonna . . . It's not meant to be sight-read. I even got a line from the violinist saying that I should rewrite it for string quartet because there's so much music in it. I mean, if I'm being told how to orchestrate my music by a lowly performer, then there's some really big problems here in the realm of composing.

But! That's the best I've gotten, is a sight-reading. In six years, I've gotten one sight-reading out of my classical music. Frank was right: the worst kind of burn. The person who asked me for it was desperate for string duo music. I never heard from Joyce Hammond again. Never. And I actually

refused to give the music to another guy in that orchestra who desperately wanted to hear and see my music because I wanted to give her first-performance rights.

It was so romantic; it was so retarded; I was so naïve. I still, to this day, have not heard that piece of music except in my synthesizer version. There is no joy in being thwarted. There is no glory in the fight well fought and lost. Especially in music. There's no point. My joy is being chosen for my voice. The last several gigs I've had had nothing to do with my voice. They were commerce, pure and simple, and desperation on the part of a person like Steve Vai, who never would have worked with me had he could have afforded the twenty thousand dollars a week that T. M. Stevens asked because he didn't want to work with him. Both T. M. Stevens and Terry Bozzio both asked for twenty thousand dollars a week. That's how worth it it would've been for them to play with Steve. Yet *I'm* doing it for seven hundred dollars a week.

That's a very, very important distinction because, if my bass playing finds its best avenue of expression in the music of Steve Vai and I'm only getting seven hundred dollars a week, then-then there's something wrong in the concept of what you deserve and what music, what music is good for and what my bass playing is right for and who is expressing the most joy from being with me every day and hearing my voice. My voice doesn't get heard, I have no point in being there.

Chapter Twenty-one

Artistry, Craftsmanship, and Low-Grade Moronism

I have two more questions, and we covered both of them, but I just wanted to clarify. Artistry versus craftsmanship: As I recall, you said Saturday that you don't view yourself as an artist. You'd rather be a— I mean, you think you could be a craftsman, but you don't even view yourself as a good craftsman because of all the so-called mistakes you made in your recorded music.

Very nice. Yes.

So is that . . . You still actually view yourself as a flawed craftsman?

No. In the two days that we've discussed this, I've totally changed my mind. You're absolutely correct: I'm an artist. The problem is that I'm one of these naïve artists, like Howard Finster, I think is his name. The guy who does the—he did that album cover for Talking Heads *[Little Creatures]*. He does all that very naïve religious imagery and stuff like that. Ahh . . . Anybody would point to him, anybody who points to him and says that he makes mistakes in his art is a damn fool. It's folk art, and if he . . . From the way he paints, it looks like if he attempted to make a chair, it would be un-sit-in-able. My bass playing is un-sit-in-able. It is not meant to functionalize the four legs of the bass-playing experience. It is folk art in the most extreme and financially remunerative fashion. Frank chose me as his local, as his spoon player. All I did was rattle around on my strings and cross my fingers and hope I didn't get fired the next week. My microphone got turned off within the first tour. And they kept it on stage for the second tour, but you can't hear my vocals in any of the road tapes.

[Laughing.] *That's what I've heard.*

Okay. Thanks a *lot*. You know, don't tell me, "Just make it look good." And I'm pretty good at that. I'm pretty good at that. I'm good at making the appearance that I am fulfilling my performance destiny, but in actuality there's, there's "agendi" all over the place. Everybody needs something else, and my needs are to have my voice be heard. And that voice is a quirky piece of shit. It is odd, and it is funky, and it is weird, and it's, in a lot of areas, very cool. And I am only pleased when, when it is . . . When am I only pleased? I am only pleased when it *works!* When the coolness and the oddity functionalize perfectly to make the music other than it was meant to be. When my voice has found its niche. When I am the cello in the string quartet of the disparate elements of the performers that are being involved in it. And there's no room for that in, in a rock band. They don't need artists in rock bands.

Rock bands need people who can play the song. And I'm a very big fan of the song being more important, but I wasn't for a very long time. I very much felt that it didn't matter if my voice was discombobulatory to the, to the song as a whole because nobody turned around and said, you know, "You're really messing things up." With Frank, I-I stayed in some pockets at some times. In other times, when I went outside of those pockets, I didn't get complaints from him. Ninety-eight percent of the time, I didn't get a complaint.

My artistry, if you choose to call it that, is in my voice being heard. That's what you hear. But it's not, it's not, it's not a *functional* art. It's decorative. And a functional bass artist is, is the perfect blend of inspiration, technique, technology. And I have none of that. I don't have technology. I don't have technique; I am sloppier than hell; I make tons of mistakes, and I can't understand why Frank would put them on records. Is he at fault? He edited out my mistakes in the first several albums' worth of things that came from the road. *Ship Arriving Too Late [to Save a Drowning Witch]*? That's twenty different cities. Each track has twenty different cities on each track, so there's probably sixty cities involved on that entire twenty-minute opus. And when he lets a major, huge clunker, like the beginning of "Rhymin' Man" [*Broadway the Hard Way*], go out, I have to question the validity of the musical process through his eyes and ears completely because there's, there's no right and wrong anymore.

Does he need a producer now? Did he need a producer when he had Bob Stone mixing all his stuff and having all the treble be so high because Frank's high-end hearing was gone, and he said, "That's exactly how I want it"? No bass in six or seven albums in a row. That's scarier to me than whether or not I'm an artist or a craftsman because I don't make chairs for people to sit in. I have, I have big, huge murals that depict certain microscopic life vistas, and that's more important than the concept of "my artistry is so supreme that it can inspire children across the world to pick up the bass and become . . . " Eh, we could have an army of improvisors and melodic geniuses cruising around and changing the face of music. If I wanted to, I would have stuck, staked that claim years ago. I would've been on every TV show going, "Why is music the same? Why are all rock bands so similar?"

And you didn't want to?

No. My voice is . . . My voice is unnecessary for that fight. Let somebody else take over that fight, if there's a fight for that. In actuality there isn't. Most music is "Thank *God!* We got a record deal!" Whose fault is it? Bass players'? Very rarely. I was very, very pleased when, for the first month of it being on the radio, I had no idea who did the song "Long View." I didn't even know what the name of the song was. All I knew was that the bass and drums are starting off this song, and the bass is not doing an amazing amount of stuff, and the tone isn't genius, but it isn't really cheesy either. And for coming out of that—what, it's a Gibson Ripper or something like that?—for coming out of that bass, that's pretty amazing. And so I was very pleased to hear the bass have this very simple, very rollicking, funky riff be the basis for this really beautiful and really crunchy song. It really, really rocks. Those guys [in Green Day] rock. I don't care what you say; they are very interesting musicians. He's a very good guitar player. He's doing stuff that nobody else is doing, and it's very microscopic, subtle stuff that I think you would probably say about me, that I don't know how I get that thing that I did, but I know I've never heard somebody do the guitar strumming that Billie Joe [Armstrong] does on "Long View." It's like a sample of a guitar *ker-chunk* in between the actual strums. I've never heard that before, and that's folk art. *That's* why they're famous. *That's* why they deserve to have sold all those millions of records. Not because he sings in a British accent and not because the songs are absolute genius. Because the songs *aren't* incredibly great. I can't really listen to them all the way through. But that song has a killer chorus, and a killer chorus is what rock and roll is all about. Nothing else matters.

Okay. Um . . . I asked you this question before, and we kind of got sidetracked. I'll try one more time. Could you explain as briefly as you can the difference between song-writing and composing? You said you're not a songwriter but a composer.

Well, did I *say* I was a composer?

No, you didn't say you were a composer; you said you'd like to be a composer.

Yes. But I'd like to be a conductor more than I'd like to be a composer.

Okay. Conductors can—

Compose? Absolutely.

So what's the difference then between composing a song and writing a song? [Thunes rears back, mouth hanging open in shock.] I mean composing and writing a song. I'm sorry. I'm sorry!

Wow! Wooooooo!

I'm sorry. It was a slip of the tongue.

Yeah, you wish. Um, we prefer, us composers prefer calling it composing *pieces.*

Yeah. I knew there was a word in there.

Yes. I'm not a composer because I don't compose all the time. I don't have the drive to express myself in structures. If I want-ed to, I would be at the piano [in German accent] oal day lung. Or in front of ze pees oaf papier, oal day lung.

That inspiration that I had was purely to experience two peo-ple sitting in a room being forced by the composer to experience themselves playing things that they find enjoyable. I specifically organized the material in this piece so that string players, either a cellist, in this case a cellist and a violinist, would have stuff that sat underneath their fingers in an interesting way that would say, "This composer thought about what he was doing. He knew exactly what would happen to us when we put this piece of music in front of us and attempted to perform it."

I organized time, but that wasn't as important as organizing events for these two musicians. And if I were to write a song, it would necessarily be interesting to the audience. This piece that I wrote was designed to be very, very interesting. Overly interesting. Complicatedly interesting to two individuals who performed on certain kinds of instruments. If I wanted to write something for the flute, I'd have to do a lot more investigatory process because I don't know shit about the flute. I don't know about overtones that much, and I don't know about fingerings that much, and if I were going to do something with fingering, it would have to be, you know, alternating keys in a certain mathematical process. Stuff like that that would be fun, that they would say, "Oh my God. This person knows what they're doing."

Elliott Carter, American composer, is the same way. He likes to do stuff that the performer says, "Wow. This was fun to play." Hindemith has always been considered very fun to play, more fun to play than to listen to. I thought this was fun to listen to for myself. I found harmonic things going on in there that I enjoyed, but it was for— It was for fingering; it was for bowing; it was for technique, and it was for interest, for the players themselves to find something humorous within the fact that somebody actually thought more about what *they* were doing than what the audience would relate to. When I played this piece for a music teacher who was also a composer, he said it sounded like a great first movement. When I tried to start a second movement that had a more generally classical form to it, doing one piece of music for a very long time and then having, you know, genesis, geneses, come through that—this piece happens in six and a half minutes—there's ten pieces of music in it. Ten distinct sections. And that's not good composition; that's very, very, very *bad* composition. But I used a couple of melodic chunks, and I tried to bring them back. That's an attempt at good composition, but I didn't compose it for it to be a good composition. I didn't compose it for it to be listenable to an audience.

I enjoyed it, and the performers would enjoy it. I haven't gotten any performers to perform it, so I don't know how much they enjoy it, but I know for a fact stuff in there is boss. Using double stops, notes against open strings, there's a compendium of violinistic and cellistic experience, technology that isn't more important than the music. It was composed to be more important than the music, but it was also composed for me to find interest in it, and there are some incandescently beautiful moments in it. They're in no way supposed to be mathematically correct or perfect. But if I tried to write this out for a rock band or do something as beautiful for a rock band, I would have to think about the interplay between the guitar and the bass. The guitar by itself is already six different strings, so that's six different voices that I would have to orchestrate for. If I got a piano in there, I would have to sit around with my four-track, which I don't own a four-track anymore, so I can't do that. Ahh . . . I haven't had a computer with a sequencer that's been functional in the past five years, so I can't do that there. It is purely enjoyable for me to listen to other people's music.

The difference between composition and songwriting is purely that songwriting is *not* composition. Songwriting is finding a good melody and good stuff underneath it. Songwriters know how to write songs; I'm not a songwriter. Composers know how to compose; I'm not a composer. But I have written songs, and I've written pieces, but I've enjoyed the writing of them more than the hearing of it because I've never heard them. They've never . . . My music has never been performed by anybody. Ever. I've spent thirty-six years never having a piece performed. Now, most songwriters play their songs to an audience. That's performance. It has been performed. End of story. Composers do everything in their power to get their pieces performed, even by string orchestras. This thing's been sitting around for six years; I've given it to six duos; I've never gotten anything in return. I

have not handed it to somebody and said, "Play my fucking music or I'm going to kill you."

My whole musical life has been one oddity after another. Everything that I've tried to do hasn't worked. And when I try to do nothing, things come to me. I'm married; I'm happy; music has found me nonuseful. Music itself has found me unnecessary. It has placed me here in happiness for the first time in years, and music hasn't made me happy, and I haven't made music happy, so there's no— There's no sadness. The music that I've done, if it's making other people happy within that period of time that I was unhappy . . . You know, most composers would be very glad to say, "My personal experience had no expression in my music at the time." Stravinsky says that all the time. Ninety-eight percent of all of his good, really happy, "up" music was performed when his wife died. His first wife, his first wife died; his daughter died; he had an ugly period in the forties. Really bad. He was sick; some horrible diseases came up, stuff like that. And he was very ill, and his music at the time was jaunty as heck, absolutely no connection whatsoever. That's composition, where the notes are more important than anything else. Songwriting, the audience's reaction is more important than anything.

How's that?

Perfect.

Thank you.

Um . . . Something else came up. That was going to be the last question, but something else came up. How important is, or was, accessibility in your playing of the bass guitar?

Meaning how much of my information satisfactorily presented itself to the ears and intellect of the audience members?

Yes. And how much thought did you put into being accessible?

Never. Never once in a second. Never. What the hell does that *mean?* As a bass player, to be accessible means to satisfy the requirements of the riff. To satisfy the requirements of the song.

To satisfy the requirements of the guitar player's fucking ego. That is the most important job 98 percent of all bass players will ever have to face because bass players aren't supposed to have ideas. They're not supposed to be geniuses. They're supposed to be functionaries. They are low— They are the lowest-level functionary. This is not a cut; this is a fact. If you are in a band like Primus, it's *your* band. If you wanna play bass like Stu Hamm, it's *your* band. Stanley Clarke. These are bass players' bands; they are supposed to be out front. They're serving a completely, utterly different purpose then. Stanley Clarke has his *own* bass player, for God's sakes. It's a completely different set of rules.

If you are a bass player in a rock band, you are by definition a moron. A low-grade moron because you are doing nothing except what the song requires, what your guitar player requires, or what the composer requires. My job was never specifically to serve the music. It was to serve Frank, and Frank had different needs at different times. And I acted like the bass moron more often than not, but the only things you're hearing on records are the pieces of expression that are different from other things that have gone on. He's not gonna put out on record every single version of "Advance Romance" he ever recorded every single night. That's where the low-level functionaryism comes in, and that's why I'm earning my money. The improvisatory freedom moments are exactly what I was able to do when nobody else was looking.

[Pause.] Where were we?

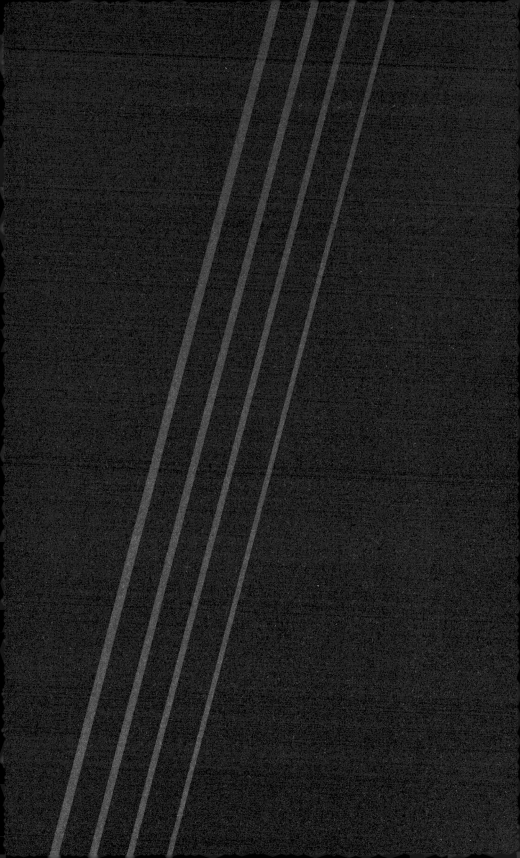

Chapter Twenty-two
Pointillism and a False Ending

Where were we? Uh . . . You answered my question.

There was something else I needed to add to that. And that was, I think . . . Searching for it . . .

Accessibility for myself would have meant how little would I have to do in order to get the message across that there was somebody inside the bass bubble, over in the corner. If at times all I needed to do was low-level functionaryism, then my bass bubble has been functional. It has been . . . I'm serving the music. Ahhh . . . Anything that . . . If I had been . . . The extreme to that would be being given a solo. When Frank gave me solos before the '88 tour, they were— Ninety-eight percent of them were within the structure of the blues song "Nigger Business," and all I have to do is play some rockin' cool stuff and I'm set. Ike Willis and Ray White came to me once in the middle of the '84 tour and said, "Why do you sound like a jazz string bass player when you're playing the solo? How do you get all that shit?" I shrugged my shoulders. I had absolutely no idea. Just having fun trying to fill up the space. I got my twenty-four bars or something like that, and, uh, and I played jazz. I played string bass. Why *shouldn't* I sound like that? But in '88, Frank had me do most of my solos against atonal, weirdly orchestrated Synclavier tracks, and all that I have to do right there is to be as pointillistic as I can to fit into the orchestral weirdness. I want to be a part of the pointillistic oddity that is going on.

Pointillistic?

Pointillism, as in . . . Artistic pointillism was [Georges] Seurat and, uh . . . Well, Seurat. He invented it. [His painting] *A Sunday Afternoon on the Island of La Grande Jatte,* where the little dots make up larger colors, like that bit in [the film] *Ferris Bueller's Day Off,* in the museum? Where they close-up on that painting, and they show the little girl's face, and it gets closer and closer and closer to the guy's eyes, and it shows the girl, and you realize it's just a bunch of little dots. Uh, musical pointillism was a name given to Webern's style. And then you got a note, you know, you've got a high flute note here, and then a cello *plunk* here, a *da-da-da-da-da,* and it supposedly makes up a musical whole. It doesn't really mean the same thing. The music itself is the point of the sounds of the instruments themselves. That's the point of the music, not to stretch "point" too far.

So you were playing these against the—

Exactly! And I was either Scott Thunes playing [sings] *doodle-doodle-duh, doodle-doodle-duh, doodle-doodle-ruh, doodle-coang-coang-coang-coang-coang,* against this music, so that there's the Scott Thunes voice, against the pointillism stuff, or I'm pretending to be this, a part of this electronic orchestra. The extreme of accessibility is it doesn't matter what I do. The music has to be served in that arena. My accessibility comes from where, if I have something to say, it gets said. And if you're in a bass solo, everybody's eyes and ears are on you, and you can do pretty much anything you want. My melodic chunks are, as far as I'm concerned, very simple. I either stay within a key or I don't. What happens if you're [guitarist] John Scofield and you start playing the next key—this is a jazz technique—you start playing the next chord you're going to, three notes before the chord changes? It's a very standard jazz technique. It's been around for hundreds of years.

If I do that, am I being weird? Am I being jazz? Am I being inaccessible? Or am I fulfilling a preformed condition of how music is? It's all there. I can pick and choose at what point I wanna do it. If I am doing something and the audience doesn't understand it, it's because the audience doesn't understand music. Now, if I'm playing with Frank and his audience . . . You've either got musical boneheads who only wanna watch the water turn black or the snow go yellow, or you've got people who think that Frank is the best modern composer for rock bands that ever was and know classical music very well. That's going to be a very small percentage of the audience, compared to the boneheads. But they both know that weirdness can happen. And if they see me playing weird stuff and they don't know that I have technique behind it, I don't care.

My accessibility is that I have been able to circumvent my stage fright; I have been able to circumvent my stomach pains; I've been able to circumvent the daggers coming from behind me to create a piece of melodic texture that deserves to be there at that point in time. But 98 percent of the time, I was scared out of my mind, and I shook my head whenever Frank pointed at me. And if he nodded at me and said, "You're *gonna* fuckin' do it," I would try and do as little as possible and have as much musical sense come out of that. And a lot of the times it happened because, as a bass player, you can get standing ovations from going [sings] *diddle-doodle-duddle-daddle-diddle-doodle-duddle-daddle,* just playing within the box ten times in a row. That's a, you know— Put the white lights on for a second. Everybody freaks out. None of that shit matters to me. It's all fake rock, and I've never been in fake rock. And when I *was* in fake rock, it immediately turned into real rock in the Dweezil band, and my accessibility came down to nil.

But! I pulled back, decided to make my money and go home. That was easy. [Long pause.]

Is there anything else you wanted to cover?

I don't think so. I have no idea where else we could go.

Okay. If a year from now, a young bass player comes up to you wherever you are and says, "I read your interview in **Bass Player;** *I bought all your albums, and you changed the way I played the bass; I'm a better player now," what would you say? He's a kid, twenty-two years old.*

Thank you very much. [Sits back, all squinty-eyed and purse-lipped, chin up and arms folded.]

Okay.

[I turn the tape player off and eject the tape, getting ready to pack my bag. Thunes suddenly says, "But he's not gonna say I changed his life!" I jam the tape back in and switch the machine on again.]

Okay, you told me this kid is not going to say you changed his life. I don't understand.

When you asked the question, you said, if a kid comes up to me and says I changed his musical life, he's a better bass player now, I would say "Thank you very much." Then I said, apparently off the record but not really, "I never tell someone that they're wrong if they tell me I was very good." "Thank you very much."

But! If you tell me I'm the best bass player you've heard, I will tell you you're wrong; you're full of shit; you've got to rethink your priorities. Because you don't know *anything* about the bass if you think that my bass playing is really great. I play *me* on the bass, and you will be reacting to me, the sound of me and my mind, meshing with the music. As a bass player, there is nothing going on that practicing scales for two months won't help you do. You could play all my riffs . . . Written out, you could play all of them—if you're a good bass player right now, if you're an intermediate bass player, you could play everything I ever played—if it was written out and you practiced it for a week. There's nothing there but the weirdness of my voice coming out at a certain time, and that . . . I'm very proud to be an addition to the voices being in music today. I'm very proud of the work I have done, but if I'm changing people's lives, it's because they're reacting to *me*. They can call it bass playing, but they are semantically incorrect.

They are hearing my voice being played on the bass, and if I turned somebody into a better bass player, all I am doing is showing them a technique—a standard technique—of scale playing or arpeggiation that they may not have had previous. And since my technique is not so exalted, they should definitely have learned that at that point. Or they are learning how to make their own voice heard. And that is the only reason that anybody should ever take lessons or listen to music that is of a technological nature. For you to listen to it only because it's technologically good, if you like songs, it doesn't matter what everybody else is doing. And you can't learn how to write a song from hearing a performance. So if you are becoming a better bass player because you are listening to me, it's because you are doing . . . Your technique is improving to a very standard level, or your voice is being heard. You're hearing your own voice coming out. And if you are not

hearing your own voice coming out and you're just sounding like somebody else, then you're not improving at all in my eyes. [Long pause.]

I see.

Do you dislike that answer?

Oh boy. It's not that I dislike it—

Does it make you uncomfortable?

Yes.

Explain.

Okay . . . It makes me uncomfortable because it seems to me that, um . . . Well, I find it difficult to accept compliments myself, but—

You say "Thank you very much." It's really easy. You give them that little smile, that enigmatic little grin that you give me; you say "Thank you very much," and they know exactly what you're thinking, and they can't say anything against it. It's very fun; it's very easy, and it's effective.

Okay, so, in that sense, you're right. You say "Thank you very much." What you said afterwards, it just strikes me as . . . It's just the inverse of saying . . . To me, you saying "I haven't done anything spectacular" is just an inverted way of saying "I'm the best in the world."

[Blows enormous raspberry.] *Pppppbbbbtttttthhhhhht!* [Laughs.] That's the funniest thing I've ever heard! What does that even *mean*?

I mean . . . I just can't believe that you think your playing is nothing except technical stuff you learned in school. That it's nothing.

I didn't *say* that! I said it is a technology, a physical, purely mechanistic technology that should be under everybody's hands. It's purely and simplistically an actual mechanical technique.

And to me, that's very similar to saying it's nothing. It's nothing! It's just something that everyone should be able to do.

Somebody should physically be able to play anything like that at any point in time if they choose to be a bass player who wants to be good. Most people don't want to be good; they just want to be able to play the bass. You don't have to have a mechanistic technique at all. You don't need to step outside the box. If you're lucky, you get to play a riff that your guitar player fucking teaches you, that steps outside of the box by one or two or three notes. If you get to play a two-octave riff in the middle of a song, you're fucking God in your universe. Your chicks will come gathering, and your free beer will flow.

But 98 percent of the time, it isn't *you* that anybody's talking about. It's not your person. Your person is more important than your bass playing, and if you want to be a bass player, you have to have a technique that is at least equal to my retarded version of genius. But my voice comes out, and that's— If you want to call that great bass playing, you're gonna have to make your own dictionary. Because that's not great bass playing; that's voice explication.

So your voice is not great bass playing. You're not a great creative force on the bass.

No. I did not extend the realm of the bass technology. No fucking way. No way in hell. Never had, never will.

So why do so many people think you have?

I have no idea. I don't know that so many people think I have.

Everyone I spoke to said that you were one of the greats.

I know that people think I'm an idiot. That's about it.

Well, maybe personally, but I'm just talking about as a bassist.

Great. Well, if they want to express into the world . . . If the energy that comes back to me is that on the one hand I'm no good for music because I'm no good for musicians, and on the other hand I'm one of the world's great bass players, you're going to have a couple of really strong arguments from me. Really heavy, really lengthy ones. Because I can't be both. I can't be good for music and bad for music at the same time. And it's been proven to me that I'm bad for music. And you may call that bitter, but it's fact. And I'm happier now than I've ever been. So! What does that mean?

I don't know.

Exactly!

You don't strike me as being particularly bitter.

Right.

You don't strike me as being particularly crazy.

Right.

I mean, you may be a great actor and might start bouncing off the walls and ceilings as soon as I leave, but—

Well, you don't get to enjoy me with my friends doing all the crazy stuff that I think is funny and that pisses other people off.

On the other hand, it just seems that, it's not posing exactly, but what is—

False modesty?

No, not false modesty. I don't know. It's like a game. You can't admit to a certain thing because then somehow somebody will be able to pin you down.

As what? As a great bass player?

Yeah.

[Wide-eyed and sarcastic.] Oh my *God*, what would happen if I admitted I was a great bass player? How would that ruin my *life?*

I don't know. And that's why I'm curious. I think it's possible for somebody to be the two things that you said are not possible. I think it's possible to say, "He's hard to get along with, and he's a great bass player."

Sure. Nothing wrong with that. Um . . . You didn't interview Gene Simmons because he's a great bass player.

No.

Mm-hmm. And that proved his point, when he was saying stars sell the magazine. Now: You are interviewing me as if I'm a great bass player, and that disturbs me greatly.

No. No!

[Collapses forward across table, chin down on chest, beckoning frantically with one hand for me to speak.] Go! Go!

It's both! A great bass player and as somebody who I pitched to my editor: "I heard from somebody, he's living in San Rafael. He says he's out of the business. You *know, I'd really like to talk to this guy because he's got a great talent and he said, 'Go to hell. I'm out of the business.'" And my editor said, "That is a **great** angle: 'I* QUIT!' *Go talk to him!" So—*

[Laughs; pounds tabletop with both fists; shouts.] BUT I DIDN'T QUIT!

*I know! I know! That's what I'm saying: that the whole thing is really bizarre because I've not met anyone who seems to know the whole story on any level. So that's why I wanted . . . So, you know, it's both: as a personality, **and** as a great bass player.*

Great bass playing can take you to the top. I'm not at the top. That means I have personality conflicts with the idea of fame and fortune, or my musical expression doesn't beget the choices that allow you to rise like cream to the top. If I rose like cream to the top, that happened when I was twenty-one; I played with Frank; there's nowhere else to go. Let's just say before anybody ever knew that I existed, I would have lost gigs merely from the fact that I played with Frank. They can't afford me. Well, obviously they can; they have; they've gotten me for free. Things change. Things are odd.

But! I've risen like cream to the top of a lifestyle that many musicians will never, ever have: happiness. Personal satisfaction. If I had the best of all possible worlds, I would have thousands of dollars' worth of musical equipment in that little room over there, and I would sit in front of the computer and either play beautiful music into it and have recordings of my music that my wife and I could enjoy, or I would actually be able to later orchestrate them and have them be performed live. I think I'd actually prefer to conduct an orchestra live quite often than to write groovy music because that's . . . Nobody knows exactly what [composer] Danny Elfman has done. Steve Bartek is my personal God, and I think that he's a better musician than Danny Elfman because he orchestrates all that shit. He finally, after ten years, has gotten his own movie, and it was some cheesy little comedy. Even Danny Elfman's first movie was not a cheesy little comedy. It was fuckin' *Pee-wee's Big Adventure,* and that was the shit.

And everything else is secondary to happiness, and I don't want to come off like some Zen, hibernating monk. It's not that I stepped down off the mountain to live in the forest.

[Side A of the second 120-minute tape is full. We've been talking for three hours without a break. I flip the tape over, asking him to stop so I won't miss anything.]

Chapter Twenty-three

Knowing When to Stop

Go on. You spent ten years?

I spent ten years in Los Angeles thinking that my three hundred dollars a week paid by Dweezil to rehearse and/or record was all that I could get, and so I was afraid to stop it and wait for another gig. Most people would remain living in their Yucca Street apartments, carrying their guitar-caseless guitar to MIT every day if they could. Three hundred dollars a week would pay for their schooling. It would pay for their beer and their cigarettes and their porno mags. It's, it's nice work if you can get it, but if I can make more being happy at home every night, working at a computer company that is doing interesting stuff in the world and is gonna teach me shit about stuff that I'm actually interested in, if I've done Frank already, where else is there to go? Okay? I could be in a really great rock band that makes a million dollars? Nobody's even hired me as a second *banana* for a really good rock band!

Josh had a really good story. I'm gonna tell his story because it probably won't get into the interview about this. He was one of ten people that was going to be going to Chicago and auditioning for the Smashing Pumpkins when they fired their drummer. He talked to this guy for several days, this agent-manager guy, and finally Josh said, "Okay. What do I do? I'm going." And the agent said, "Okay. We've found a couple of plane trips for you, and it's gonna cost you about fifteen hundred, twelve hundred dollars round-trip." And Josh said, *"What?!"* "Yeah, but you get a chance to be *Smashing Pumpkins' drummer!!"* And if Josh had an interest in that, in being in a rich and famous rock band, it would be worth twelve hundred dollars for him to gamble that. But there are ten guys playing the same gamble, and the chances of something like that coming to fruition are not just one in ten. There's all sorts of other things that can happen as well. And you just . . . It just doesn't matter at some point. My friend [drummer] Carla Azar turned down—or she told me she turned down—Bruce Springsteen for ten thousand dollars a week. She wasn't interested in his music. Where is the top?

[Half minute of silence. We stare at each other. Thunes looks exhausted and bleary-eyed, exactly the way I feel.]

So there we go.

Wow. Yeah, well, I won't be interviewed at all. I was not going to do this.

That's what I heard.

I wasn't going to do this at all. When Mike called me up . . . He called Marty up, and Marty called me up. I didn't even return Mike's phone call. Just not interested at all.

And you didn't return mine for a couple days.

There was no point. What was going to happen? I was going to get two or three questions about what it was like to play with Frank. I was maybe going to get a Steve or Dweezil angle, and that would be self-serving to your magazine and not to me. And the interviews I've done in Europe have been pretty neutral. I happened to be there with Steve. I did an interview in Japan, and it's not like they asked me all about Frank, but I was very happy to answer questions about Frank. I loved Frank. And nobody thought it was weird that something else was going on besides; you know, I go over there with Steve Vai, and I get interviewed about Frank. When Dweezil was interviewed in France by this one person, they said, "Well, actually, we're just doing a paper on Frank, and we knew that this would be the only way that we could get to you."

The first thing you think of is, "*Their* needs are being served." I couldn't even begin to imagine why somebody would want to interview me in the first place because I have been interviewed already, and all that stuff has been said. The story of my life has been said; the story of the '88 tour has been said, and why would anybody actually be interested in what happened to me? Because my story is not anywhere near as bad as people who've lost everything. I never had anything to lose. I've always been searching for happiness. I've found it. I'm not in a cult. I'm happily married. She doesn't rule my life. Everything is pretty fucking mellow. I'm living in a really beautiful place with beautiful people, surrounded by my friends. I was in Los Angeles, going absolutely bananas because I couldn't understand why I couldn't get a gig. Where's the complication? And of course, why would anybody want to interview a happy person?

So have you changed your mind, or do you wish you hadn't given the interview?

No, I just wish I had the whole magazine and a cover and a byline that would explain, you know, this is a lesson to musicians everywhere, not just bass players. Because music is more important than just one small aspect of it, which is either fame or personal satisfaction in your music or anything like that. Most people don't deserve to get the musical experience that they do. I was never in a rich and famous rock band. Is that more of a shame than if I were the exact same person I am now, with the exact same melodic expression, and I never got to play with Frank? Would that be sad? Would that be weird? Would it be potluck? You never know about this shit, and everything is secondary to happiness, and I've only learned that in the last couple of years.

I was very, very pleased to be in Los Angeles, living in a very nice apartment with beautiful girlfriends and wife and playing a little bit of Dweezil's music. And I was definitely shooting fish in a barrel. I was sitting around with nothing else to do except

being paid to play music. It was other people's music, and my expressionistic needs were not being met. And I had a smile on my face every day. Or I didn't. I was very depressed, but I went through my job with as much aplomb as I could. And that's what everybody else is looking for. They just want to be in a rock band. They want their musical ideas to be valid. I'd rather have my life be valid than my musical ideas.

I think that's about it.

Making a big production out of it, I packed my tape recorder away. I was afraid we'd start up again, and I didn't want to dilute what I already had. Scott said he wanted me to hear some classical CDs before I left, so we went into his living room. I sat on the floor and listened as he explained what was going on in various pieces composed and performed by Bartók, among others. When we finished with the CDs, he went over to one of his two pianos and plunked out selections from a few more of his favorite compositions, singing along in a soft tenor. He then brought in his battered '63 Fender Precision Bass, his main axe, and handed it to me, saying that recording engineers were always amazed by its great tone. I persuaded him to put on the two Zappa CDs I'd brought with me, which he'd claimed he hadn't heard in three years. We listened to several tracks, Scott leaning back in his chair and playing air bass, his legs jerking violently in time with the music, a wide, completely genuine smile on his face.

"See! Listen to this!" he'd yell, reviewing various parts again and again to show me how he'd screwed up or deviated from the proper line. I pointed out a spot in "Oh No," from *Make a Jazz Noise Here,* where Zappa in his guitar solo echoed a riff that Scott had just played, and he said, "I never noticed that before." He began going to his closet and bringing out more CDs one at a time. We listened to the album he'd made with Fear, one of the Andy Prieboy records, and the multi-instrumental track he'd done for the Trace Elliot Amplifiers compilation CD *Also Available in Green.* After an hour and a half, I told him I had to leave.

I felt as if I'd gone at least three days without sleep and wondered how I'd make the long drive back to San Francisco.

Thunes walked me to my car, his face all puckered up behind sunglasses held together with safety pins instead of screws. I reminded him of our first phone conversation and his prediction that I'd hate his guts by the end of the interview. "Did I say that?" he asked. I nodded. "What a stupid, useless, pathetic thing to say," he mumbled.

In the parking lot, he surprised me—terrified me, actually—by giving me a long hug, whispering "Come back again soon" in my ear. As I warmed up my engine, I watched him stride away, people scattering like pigeons on the sidewalk in front of him. I expected him to turn and wave, but he marched the two blocks to his house, tramped up the stairs, and went inside without looking back.

Coda

Before I submitted the finished article, I mailed a copy to Scott because he'd asked if he could make sure that I'd gotten everything right. He sent me a computer printout a few days later, a list of "errata" he wanted corrected. It arrived in a heavy, cream-colored envelope from the Hyde Park Hotel in London, adorned with a Marilyn Monroe stamp and a Los Angeles postmark. In the empty space below poor Marilyn, Scott had drawn an obese, naked body extending down from under her perfect breasts, its buttocks twisted sideways and a bloody, dripping knife in one hand. His suggested changes were shockingly reasonable, and in jagged ballpoint at the bottom of the list, he'd written, "This was The Best fucking interview I've ever read. Not long enough. You are GOD. Everybody thinks you write Godlike."

About two months after the interview—"Requiem for a Heavyweight?"—was published in the March '97 issue of *Bass Player*, I was given the opportunity to see videotape of Frank Zappa's 1988 tour, footage taken in Barcelona and broadcast live on Spanish television. It was oddly satisfying to put faces on the various band members, especially the ones who'd had the most problems with Thunes. I looked hard for signs of tension, but all was seamless and professional, everybody smiling, laughing, and interacting like old friends. There wasn't the slightest hint of despair or performance-eroding angst.

I should probably confess here that I'd never liked Zappa. I'd found his bottomless hostility chilling, his so-called satire rudimentary and embarrassing. I'd always thought of him as just another woman-hating, defecation-obsessed American male, so I was never interested in learning more about his work. The CDs and videos I'd studied before the interview had already proven that he'd in fact written some terrific stuff, but the Barcelona show utterly confirmed my misjudgment. Except for the smutty lyrics and tedious in-jokes, I loved what I heard.

Impressed as I was with the group as a whole, I was blown away by the superhuman brilliance of Thunes. His range and originality were almost magical, his playing as near to perfection as I could imagine. The only glitch came when he was to execute a solo. He must have resisted at first because Zappa aimed his finger, nodded firmly, and mouthed something like, "Yes, you *will*," before an anxious-looking Scott complied, firing off a clanking, pointillistic salvo of notes. It was his only flicker of hesitation; despite the stage fright and stomach pains, the anger and disillusionment, his voice—a vehicle of astonishing beauty and transcendent emotion—dominated the entire concert.

It really *was* the best band I'd never heard in my life, and Scott Thunes was without question one of the world's greatest musicians. I watched the tape three times in a row and fell into a severe depression that lasted weeks.

Discographies

Gene Simmons

ALBUMS: **With Kiss** *Kiss* [Casablanca]; *Hotter Than Hell* [Casablanca]; *Dressed to Kill* [Casablanca]; *Alive!* [Casablanca]; *Destroyer* [Casablanca]; *Rock and Roll Over* [Casablanca]; *Love Gun* [Casablanca]; *Alive II* [Casablanca]; *Dynasty* [Casablanca]; *Unmasked* [Casablanca]; *Music from the Elder* [Casablanca]; *Creatures of the Night* [Casablanca]; *Lick It Up* [Mercury]; *Animalize* [Mercury]; *Asylum* [Mercury]; *Crazy Nights* [Mercury]; *Hot in the Shade* [Mercury]; *Revenge* [Mercury]; *Alive III* [Mercury]; *Unplugged* [Mercury]; *Carnival of Souls* [Mercury]; *Psycho Circus* [Mercury].

COMPILATIONS: **With Kiss** *The Originals* [Casablanca]; *Double Platinum* [Casablanca]; *Killers* [Casablanca]; *Smashes, Thrashes, & Hits* [Mercury]; *You Wanted the Best, You Got the Best* [Mercury]; *Greatest Kiss* [Mercury].

SOLO ALBUM: *Gene Simmons* [Casablanca].

Peter Hook

ALBUMS: **With Joy Division** *Unknown Pleasures* [Qwest]; *Closer* [Qwest]; *Preston Warehouse, 28 February 1980* (live) [Pilot]. **With New Order** *Movement* [Factory]; *Power, Corruption, and Lies* [Qwest]; *Low Life* [Qwest]; *Brotherhood* [Qwest]; *Technique* [Qwest]; *Live 1987 Tour* [Alex]; *BBC Radio 1 Live* [Import]; *Republic* [Qwest]; *Live in Concert* [ROIR]. **With Revenge** *Gun World Porn* [Warner Bros.]; *One True Passion* [Capitol]. **With Monaco** *Music for Pleasure* [Polydor]; *Monaco*

[Papillon/Chrysalis]. **With the Durutti Column** *Sex and Death* [Factory Too]. **With Warsaw** *Warsaw* [Import].

COMPILATIONS: **With Joy Division** *Still* [Qwest]; *Divine* [Pinnacle]; *The Peel Sessions* [Strange Fruit]; *Substance* [Qwest]; *4 CD Box Set* [Alex]; *Warsaw* [Intermusic]; *Permanent* [Warner Bros.]; *Heart and Soul* (box set) [London]. **With New Order** *Substance* [Qwest]; *The Peel Sessions* [Strange Fruit]; *The Very Best of New Order* [Alex]; *(The Best of) New Order* [Qwest]; *(The Rest of) New Order* [London]; *(The Rest of) New Order (Remixes)* [Phantom].

SOUNDTRACK: **With New Order** *Salvation* [4AD].

Jerry Casale

ALBUMS: **With Devo** *Q: Are We Not Men? A: We Are Devo!* [Warner Bros.]; *Duty Now for the Future* [Warner Bros.]; *Freedom of Choice* [Warner Bros.]; *Dev-O Live* (mini-album) [Warner Bros.]; *New Traditionalists* [Warner Bros.]; *Oh No! It's Devo* [Warner Bros.]; *Shout* [Warner Bros.]; *Total Devo* [Enigma]; *Now It Can Be Told (Devo at the Palace 12/9/88)* [Enigma]; *Smooth Noodle Maps* [Enigma]; *DEV-O Live (Expanded)* [Warner Bros.]. **With David Byrne** *Feelings* [Warner Bros.].

COMPILATIONS: **With Devo** *Hardcore Devo 1974-1977, Volumes I & II* [Rykodisc]; *E-Z Listening Disc* [Rykodisc]; *The Greatest Hits* [Warner Bros.]; *The Greatest Misses* [Warner Bros.]; *Devo Live: The Mongoloid Years* [Rykodisc]; *Hot Potatoes: The Best of Devo* [Virgin]; *Adventures of the Smart Patrol* [Discovery]; *Greatest Hits* [BMG]; *Devo Live* [Rhino Handmade]; *Pioneers Who Got Scalped (The Anthology)* [Rhino]; *Recombo DNA* [Rhino Handmade].

Scott Thunes

ALBUMS: **With Frank Zappa** *Ship Arriving Too Late to Save a Drowning Witch* [Rykodisc]; *Man from Utopia* [Rykodisc]; *Does Humor Belong in Music?* [Rykodisc]; *Them or Us* [Rykodisc]; *Jazz from Hell* [Rykodisc]; *Guitar* [Rykodisc]; *Broadway the Hard Way* [Rykodisc]; *The Best Band You Never Heard in Your Life*

[Rykodisc]; *Make a Jazz Noise Here* [Rykodisc]. **With Zappa's Universe** *Zappa's Universe* [Rykodisc]. **With Dweezil Zappa** *Havin' a Bad Day* [Barking Pumpkin]; *My Guitar Wants to Kill Your Mama* [Barking Pumpkin]; *Confessions* [Barking Pumpkin]; *What the Hell Was I Thinking?* [Barking Pumpkin]. **With Z** *Shampoo Horn* [Barking Pumpkin]. **With the Vandals** *Fear of a Punk Planet* [Triple X]. **With Western Vacation** *Western Vacation* [Muffin]; *VibraudoBlast* [MRP]. **With Andy Prieboy** . . . *Upon My Wicked Sons* [Doctor Dream]; *Sins of Our Fathers* [Doctor Dream]. **With the Waterboys** *Dream Harder* [Geffen]. **With Mike Keneally** *Hat* [Immune]. **With Seven Skys** *Waves and Tides* [Zero]. **With Wayne Kramer** *Dangerous Madness* [Epitaph]. **With Fear** *Have Another Beer with Fear* [Fear/Sector 2]. **With Cynthia Jane** *Lo and Behold* [H. H. Smythe]. **With Anthony Hindson** *It's a Curious Life* [Wind in Hare]. **With Geoff Wolf and John Hanes** *Aviator* [Geoscott].

COMPILATIONS: **With Frank Zappa** *You Can't Do That on Stage Anymore, Vols. I, III, IV, V, and VI* [Rykodisc]. **With Trace Elliot Amplifiers** *Also Available in Green* (one track) [Trace Elliot].

SOUNDTRACK: **With Andy Prieboy** *Blood and Concrete* (two tracks) [Capitol].

Photo Credits

About the Author

Thomas Wictor is a contributing editor for *Bass Player*. Before he turned to music journalism, he was a stevedore, a bartender, an English teacher, a technical writer, a proofreader, a voice-over actor, a bar musician, a delivery driver, and a document retriever. He lives in Southern California.